MINDS IN MANY PIECES

MINDS IN MANY PIECES

The Making of a Very Special Doctor

By Ralph Allison, M.D.

with Ted Schwarz

Rawson, Wade Publishers, Inc.

New York

Library of Congress Cataloging in Publication Data

Allison, Ralph.
Minds in many pieces.

1. Allison, Ralph. 2. Psychiatrists—United States—Biography. I. Schwarz, Ted, joint author.
II. Title.
RC339.52.A44A35 1980 616.89'0092'4 [B] 78-65420
ISBN 0-89256-097-5

Published simultaneously in Canada by McClelland and Stewart, Ltd.
Manufactured in the United States of America by
R.R. Donnelley & Sons, Crawfordsville, Indiana
Designed by E. O'Connor
First Edition

To my wife, Mitzi, and our children, who have stood by me throughout the trials and tribulations of my career

All patients' names and identifying characteristics have been changed to protect their privacy.

Contents

MINDS IN MANY PIECES

Chapter 1

The Molding of a Psychiatrist

Santa Cruz, California, was a small coastal community when I established my psychiatric practice there in the early 1960s. The few thousand year-round residents were mostly quiet people whose main source of livelihood came from the summer tourists who flocked to the area's high mountains and towering redwood trees. The community was barely touched by the riots and dissension that rocked the rest of the state during that era of political and social upheaval. The residents were friendly and more concerned with day-to-day living than with issues such as the Vietnam War and racial integration. It was an ideal place to settle and raise a family. And the psychiatric problems I encountered there were, for the most part, fairly routine.

There were housewives depressed by the way their lives were unfolding, who were desperately seeking a sense of purpose and personal identity. There were people whose self-hatred was so strong that they wondered why they should go on living. And there were patients whose misconceptions made them feel as though others were out to harm them, although they had families and friends. These people might have been found in psychiatrists' or psychologists' offices anywhere in the country.

The only unusual cases I encountered in those first few months were the problems of indigent hippies who had come to Santa Cruz in search of a miracle. These troubled young people were unwilling or unable to cope with life without artificial supports. They drank heavily, used a variety of drugs, and never found the inner peace and happiness they so craved. Some committed suicide. Others were committed to state mental hospitals. The rest sought professional help, and a number of them found their way into my office.

All in all, my psychiatric practice was varied and interesting, but not unusual, and my life followed this routine for almost ten years. Patients came to see me with what they thought were unique, insurmountable problems, unaware that I had heard similar stories many times from other people. I showed them the alternatives they had and helped them to see the value of their lives by using established psychiatric techniques.

Sometimes treatment lasted only one or two sessions. Often it might continue for several months. More often than not, treatment was successful and I congratulated myself on the skills I had developed. I had learned how to draw out patients' deeper, often unconscious, emotions and thereby get to the root of their problems. Depression, for example, is frequently the result of anger that has been internalized. Once a patient can learn to admit his or her anger, I can help the person find a way to express and deal with the anger in a healthy manner. When the anger is eliminated, the depression disappears. The patient may have felt the results bordered on the miraculous, but the techniques were routine for a psychiatrist.

Because I had spent so many years practicing fairly traditional psychiatry, I had lost sight of the fact that the working of the mind was still very much an unknown territory, indeed, more of a mystery than any other facet of human existence.

Outer space has been called man's last frontier. Every year we spend millions of dollars developing complex electronic probes that are rocketed toward distant planets. We are all aware of man's search for answers to the mysteries of distant galaxies, yet few are cognizant of the probing of a far more important, equally unknown "wilderness" area. Every day a different type of explorer uses words, reason, and instinct in an attempt to understand the complexities of an expanse as vast as all infinity and as compact as the human brain. This is the territory of the mind in which are contained all the horrors, joys, fears, happiness, and seemingly limitless powers we can experience.

I was soon forced to confront the fact that psychiatric "science" was still in its infancy. Through a variety of circumstances I became an explorer of this second "frontier." And I discovered that many of the comfortable assumptions I had held about psychiatry were questionable. More important, I discovered how much I still had to learn, how much uncharted territory there still was.

In my role as explorer I witnessed parapsychological phenomena for which there is, as yet, no satisfactory explanation. And I talked and worked with more than forty-five unique individuals, each of whom had several different "persons" living in one body. Although my comfortable routine had ended, I was soon to be faced with the greatest challenge of my career.

The results of my explorations into the mind were beyond my wildest imaginings back during those early years. I would soon find myself exposed to one of the rarest of all mental illnesses—multiple personality. It was the disease made famous in two books, *The Three Faces of Eve* and *Sybil,* both of which also became popular films. So little is known about this abnormality that, at the time, a doctor had to innovate treatment whose success or failure could mean life or death for the patient. Tragically, I was not always successful, but my knowledge grew to the point where I found myself thrust into international prominence. I gave a series of lectures on the subject in Sweden. I led medical education courses on multiple personality for the American Psychiatric Association's annual meetings. I hold such titles as Fellow of the American Psychiatric Association and Past Chairman, Department of Psychiatry for Dominican Santa Cruz Hospital; I have membership in the Society For Experimental & Clinical Hypnosis and numerous other memberships.

Despite my prominence and success, I am still a student in the field. My cases and experiences have made it clear that our knowledge of the mind, no matter how great, is still just a tiny fragment of what it could be. There is an infinite world within our heads and we are just beginning to probe its secrets.

I realized for the first time how mysterious and complex the mind was during my psychiatric residency at Stanford Medical Center in California. I was new there, having previously completed an internship in Highland–Alameda County Hospital and served two years as a flight surgeon in the U.S. Air Force. During that period I encountered people with all sorts of emotional problems. Some were extremely anxious about their marriages and family relationships. Others were in what is known as a catatonic state—they had become so depressed that they mentally withdrew from the world. Many catatonic patients say nothing, do nothing, and generally respond like robots when they do react at all. Yet even these cases had not prepared me for David.

I first met David in the spring of 1960 at a table in the psychiatric ward of the medical center. I was eating lunch with the patients instead of using the hospital staff cafeteria. It was something the psychiatric ward doctors were encouraged to do. Such closeness at lunch was supposed to create a more relaxed atmosphere in the ward. The patients were more likely to view us as friends in whom they could confide their problems. A psychiatrist, even one only recently out of school like myself, is frequently viewed as an authority figure much like a patient's father or mother. Since many of the patients' problems stemmed from their relationships with their parents, the head of the psychiatric ward felt it was important for the doctors to be viewed less formally.

David, who had entered the ward the previous day, was a huge bear of a man. He was well over six feet tall and weighed at least 250 pounds. He had been working as a substitute teacher in a private school while studying to earn his state credentials as a full-time teacher. He was extremely bright and seemed to feel that teaching was not quite what he should be doing with his life. His grandparents were world-famous as business innovators and he had been raised to believe that he had to achieve great prominence. Anything less meant he was no good at all—a terrible psychological burden for anyone to bear.

Easter was approaching, a holiday that usually triggered David's irrational behavior. In his unbalanced mind he believed he was the greatest person on Earth—Jesus Christ—and he didn't want to be crucified.

Before entering Stanford, David had been at the state hospital under the care of Dr. Benjamin Cohen, who had an excellent reputation as a psychiatrist. David was hostile toward Dr. Cohen from their first meeting. However, the situation became disastrous when David learned that his psychiatrist was Jewish. One day when David was sitting with a group of patients, all of whom were talking about Dr. Cohen, David looked around and said ominously, "One of you will betray me!" A few hours later he met Dr. Cohen in the hall. David had been thinking about Easter and the trial he knew he, as Jesus, would face at the hands of the Romans. He thought of the Last Supper, Judas, and any number of other matters that seemed perfectly logical to his troubled mind. He became enraged, grabbed Dr. Cohen, and threw him across the hall. The doctor was not seriously hurt but David refused to continue treatment with him.

After David left the state hospital, he decided to pick his own psychiatrist. He selected me and I admitted him to Stanford as a private patient.

I was uneasy about David, though I didn't dislike him. He was actually quite personable. But David was an unusually strong individual under normal circumstances, and when he became violent, anything could happen. I didn't want him to become angry with me.

David was a paranoid schizophrenic, and his moods alternated between extreme depression and the conviction that he was the greatest person on earth. I prescribed medication to help control his mood swings, then began working with him to try to convince him to accept himself as he was. He needed to respect his own values and achievements rather than trying to live up to some ideal his family might have liked.

I was still somewhat inexperienced at this time and was delighted when David told me he had come to realize, through our therapy sessions together, that he wasn't Jesus Christ. "I know who I am and I'm ashamed I ever said I was Jesus," he told me solemnly. "How I could ever consider myself the son of God is beyond me. I've been such a fool."

I smiled delightedly as I watched him continue down the hall of the psychiatric ward. David was one of the most seriously disturbed patients under my care at the time and I had been able to reach him! Helping others had been a lifelong goal of mine and here was positive proof that my efforts were succeeding. What insight I must have shown when talking to him! What brilliantly persuasive logic I must have used! What . . .

"Stop your daydreaming, Dr. Allison," said Millie Harkness, one of the ward nurses, who was far more experienced with mental patients than most of the doctors who worked there. "I heard David in the recreation area. He doesn't think he's Jesus Christ anymore because he's convinced himself that he's really Saint Peter." And she was right.

Gradually, I convinced David that *he* was a valuable person and didn't have to be Jesus Christ or Saint Peter. He was able to leave the hospital and return to work, although he still needed periodic counseling. He took a position as a teacher and did such an excellent job that at the end of the first six weeks, the principal complimented him on his work. At that moment we learned that David wasn't quite ready to accept himself fully as a normally competent individual. He still felt he had to reach a level close to perfection.

"Yes, I did do a good job teaching during these six weeks," he reportedly told the principal. "In fact, I've been watching the other teachers and I recognize that I'm the best teacher in this school, this system, and, if I may be so immodest as to tell the truth, the best teacher in the nation! I am an educator's educator! I am . . ." David was confined to the hospital that afternoon.

David faced an additional problem as well. His parents were alcoholics who only stopped drinking when their son's mental state was at its worst. They wanted to help him through those unusually troubled times and their love for him gave them the strength to stay off the bottle temporarily. Subconsciously, David felt he had to stay sick in order to keep his parents from drinking.

When I last saw David, at the end of my stay at Stanford, he was leading a normal, controlled life. He had earned his teaching credentials but realized he couldn't yet stand the stress of being praised. He began accepting only short-term substitute jobs where his high skills would not be so noticeable and he wouldn't be praised. Later he decided he couldn't handle the pressures of teaching and obtained a steady job with routine work in an office mail room. He was using a combination of self-understanding gained through therapy and tranquilizing medication to maintain a calm, even state of mind.

I learned a lot from David, about both psychiatry and myself. Those early years of my residency were both a learning and a growth period for me. And sometimes that growth was quite painful.

Shana was a good example of one of my more embarrassing experiences. I met her when I was working in the hospital's out-patient clinic. Shana had emotional problems but was able to hold down a secretarial job and live at home. She didn't need to be hospitalized but she did need regular sessions with a psychiatrist. She would visit the clinic for counseling once or twice a week, usually at five o'clock, after she had finished work at a nearby office.

The first time I saw Shana I needed every bit of the professionalism drilled into me by my professors during the long years of college and medical school. She was very attractive. Her low-cut blouse revealed an ample bust and her miniskirt accented her narrow waist and attractive legs. I found her appearance unnerving, and I would rather have met her over a drink in a singles' club. But I was also a happily married man with a young family at the time!

Shana's problems began when her boyfriend abandoned her after she became pregnant. Her depression was compounded by her decision to have an abortion and the guilt she felt after it was over. Much of her talk was about her sex life with her boyfriend and I must admit to an occasional unprofessional thought. After all, psychiatrists are human beings, too, though we don't always like to admit that fact.

After two or three sessions I realized that Shana wasn't being completely open with me. She talked about work, dating, her apartment—everything except what was really bothering her.

While Shana talked, I tried to maintain an air of professionalism. This meant that I rocked back and forth on my chair, my hands pressed together on my lap. Periodically I would make a note on her chart. The rest of the time I nodded my head and mumbled such brilliant comments as, "Uh-huh" and "What happened next?" and "I see. Then what took place?"

The problem was that my chair wasn't really meant for rocking. During one session I accidentally leaned back a little too far, knocking the precariously positioned chair off balance. The chair flew out from under me and I found myself painfully on my back, staring up at the ceiling.

I was humiliated. The image a psychiatrist creates is all-important when treating a patient. Shana seemed to need an all-wise, totally objective, emotionally stable individual to counsel her. I wasn't certain how well I had been projecting this image but I knew that no matter how I had appeared to her before, I had completely blown it now!

I rolled over on my side in what I hoped was a graceful motion. I rose to my feet, picked up the chair, and calmly sat down. "As you were saying?" I said, my voice cracking like an adolescent's. But if Shana noticed, she was kind enough not to mention it.

When I was settled again, Shana suddenly began to talk. But instead of the evasiveness that had marked earlier conversations, she told me what had really troubled her over the years. She talked about her childhood, her doubts, her fears, her conflicts with parents, teachers, friends, and her own moral values. By the time her session was over for that day, I had gained insights into Shana that I knew would help me get her through therapy quickly and successfully. I had also made an ass of myself rocking in the chair, a fact I thought I had better discuss with her on the next visit.

When Shana entered my office the following week, I was anxious to learn if the incident had bothered her. I knew that it was essential for a therapist to bring feelings out in the open right at the start. Only then can you analyze those feelings and restore the relationship to the proper level of professionalism. Thus, I immediately asked her what she had thought of my fall the previous week.

Shana smiled, blushing slightly. "Well, Doctor," she began. "I was so embarrassed for you. I mean, when you got up and tried to go on like nothing happened, I knew you really were upset and couldn't do much talking. I felt like I had to fill all that talk space, so I just had to pour out all the things that were in me. I told you things I'd been too scared to bring up before. I mean, I wasn't frightened of your reaction anymore because I knew you weren't in a position to really say anything. I just poured out my heart and finally got through everything that was bothering me. I guess I finally fulfilled my part of the relationship the way I should have done right from the start of these counseling sessions."

Then Shana shattered my ego once again. She told me that she wished I wouldn't respond to her questions by saying, "And what do you mean by that?" as I had been taught. When she asked me a question, she wanted an answer rather than another question.

Of course, Shana didn't know those techniques were part of my psychiatric training. The doctor is supposed to be a skilled listener who encourages the patient to do all the talking. The patient is supposed to be the object of analysis, so we are trained to search for hidden meanings in his or her words. At least, that's what we were taught in school.

But Shana reminded me that a patient is indeed a human being with thoughts, feelings, and a desire for some sort of human relationship with the therapist. I had been treating her like a rat in the cage of an experimental laboratory. She taught me to become sensitive to my patients and care for them as people. A psychiatrist can reveal feelings and emotions without losing objectivity or the ability to help. Too many doctors forget this.

Part of my difficulty in revealing more of myself to Shana was probably the result of an incident that occurred while I was still in medical school at the University of California at Los Angeles.

As a new psychiatric student, I had to visit one of the mental health clinics in Los Angeles and interview a patient. We students went once a week, seeing the same patient each time so we could get an in-depth understanding of his or her case. Then we would go into a conference room at the clinic and discuss the case with other students and our psychoanalyst instructor.

My first patient was a woman named Renatta. She was young, married, and had moved to Los Angeles from New York, a city she hated.

Fortunately for me, Renatta liked to talk. I had limited interviewing skills at that time and don't know how I would have handled the type of patient who needs to be drawn out by the therapist. The only problem was that Renatta's complaints related to her sex life. At the time I had almost no sexual experience, like most of my classmates. We were all so busy studying and, in many cases, working part-time jobs to get through school, that few serious relationships or even "one-night stands" developed during this period. I had a thorough knowledge of sex, but it was clinical rather than physical—until Renatta.

At one session she mentioned that she had had an affair with a man she met while her husband was away for a few days. She proceeded to describe their night in bed together in exquisite detail. She started with the length of the man's penis—several *feet* longer than her husband's, if her description was to be believed. Then she proceeded to describe exactly what they had done together in detail that would have made a pornographer envious. I had never even realized that two people could do some of the things Renatta described, although the more I thought about it, the more interesting the ideas became. By the time she had talked herself out, I was red-faced, perspiring, and exhausted. I immediately went before my professor and fellow classmates to relate the wonders I had heard and describe the diagnostic breakthrough I thought I had achieved.

My professor was an interesting man. He was extremely short, probably less than five feet tall. He sat on the smallest chair in the room yet his legs dangled loosely over the side. They didn't reach the ground. He was completely bald and his expression was a mask of indifference. It was impossible to tell what he was thinking when you talked to him. He was also an extremely brilliant man who could quickly and accurately analyze any situation.

The professor listened to my account and nodded knowingly. I concluded with my brilliant diagnosis that the poor woman was sexually frustrated. Her husband was obviously an inadequate lover, probably because he wasn't blessed with the genitals of the stud in whose arms she had found happiness and a whole lot of other things. Then the professor quietly said, "You found her story sexually quite gratifying, didn't you? You let yourself get aroused instead of trying to understand her."

I was crushed. I had to sit and listen to the professor discuss at least a half dozen possible causes for Renatta's problems, none of which were related to her husband's genitals. He explained that her affair could be the result of earlier rejection in childhood. I was fixating on sex but Renatta was probably engaging in sex because of serious problems that had nothing to do with her husband's bedroom performance.

I only saw Renatta a few more times, then another student took my place. We were rotated on a regular basis and my time was up. Fortunately, she did receive the counseling she needed for her real problems.

Renatta's case was a painful lesson about doctor-patient involvement and professional discipline. And I didn't improve my skills by turning to the opposite extreme and developing a coldly detached manner with Shana. I'm very grateful that she managed to show me that I could be both human and professionally objective at the same time.

Experiences like these have made the practice of psychiatry particularly rich and rewarding. And I consider myself very fortunate in my choice of profession, especially since my motivation for entering the field was rather unscientific.

The students in my medical school were highly competitive. Most came from colleges where only the very best were able to go on to medical school. Competition was so fierce that some students took to sabotaging the laboratory projects of other students to make their own lab skills look better. The administration became so concerned about this vicious battle for top grades that they stopped giving any grades. Students either passed or failed their courses but they never learned their exact marks. Grades were kept and filed with the students' records because of state requirements, but a special effort was necessary to find out what they were. This practice successfully changed the atmosphere of the classes and made it possible for everyone to concentrate on learning, the real reason we were all there.

Just prior to the abandonment of traditional grading, I had received my semester report. One of my favorite courses was psychiatry, a required course for all doctors. I discovered I had gotten an "A" in the psychiatry course and figured that if I did that well, it would be worth majoring in the field. My reasoning was neither noble nor well thought out, but I have never regretted the decision.

Although my choice of psychiatry may have been somewhat haphazard, in many ways it was inevitable that I would choose a profession dedicated to serving others. The men in my family have a history of such service dating back to the earliest English settlements in this country. My full name is Ralph Brewster Allison and one of my ancestors was the Elder William Brewster who came over on the *Mayflower*. He was a minister, as were numerous others in the family, including my grandfather and father.

My father's approach to religion, and life in general, has always troubled me. He was a Presbyterian whose devotion to the church was total, and he spent many years serving as a missionary in the Philippines. He disliked emotionalism in religion and mistrusted highly emotional groups like the Pentecostals. His faith was a type of intellectual Presbyterianism that allowed him to read and write learned dissertations on matters of theology, none of which appealed to emotion. He completely ignored the concept of spirit possession, with which I would one day have to deal in my practice. He was more concerned with adapting Bible teachings to today's world to make Scripture a practical handbook for daily living.

I had always been rather intimidated by my father as I was growing up, especially when listening to his sermons each Sunday. The Presbyterian church service is always planned around the sermon. It is the high point of the Sunday program and my father worked extremely hard throughout the week planning it. Preaching that carefully worded sermon was almost his reason for "being" as a minister. All other church operations were secondary to that function in his eyes.

My father was also a very troubled man. He had many social and financial problems, which resulted in a great deal of unexplained family tension. It was only as an adult that I became aware of some of the problems, and only recently that I learned why we children had not shared in an understanding of the source of those problems. My father believed that if he expressed his real concerns in front of his children, it would be traumatically damaging to our maturing minds. He believed that good fathers don't burden their children with their problems.

Naturally, we children knew father was upset because he was depressed all the time. This silence and isolation troubled and intimidated us, perhaps having the very effect he thought would occur if he was open with us. In any case, only my mother was allowed to share any of his burdens.

To make matters worse, my father had, and still has, the habit of silence. He can sit silently for hours in a room filled with people, immersed in a magazine. He has often done it in my home, a fact which upsets my wife. Yet he does not feel he is being rude; he simply chooses to avoid communication.

Even today I find this conversational barrier difficult to adjust to. Recently, I spent a week with my father and I had dozens of questions I wanted to discuss with him. My wife and children were out of town and I was looking forward to the time together to learn more about him. I wondered what he had been like as a boy. I wanted to know about his father, also a Presbyterian minister, his brothers and sisters, and all the influences which led to his development. He didn't talk to me however; he spent his time buried in reading matter. When we went out to eat I was able to ask some questions, but he still would not discuss anything with me. Instead, he gave me a sermon, which was and is his only means of communication. I still have trouble dealing with this fact even though, as an adult, I recognize that he treats everyone the same way.

My father has always made it a point to avoid living and preaching by a rigid set of theological "rules." His father, my grandfather, had been a typical "hellfire and brimstone" preacher who fervently believed there was a "right" way to live if you wanted to be saved. Mother felt this was why my father turned away from rigid dogma.

The result of my father's feelings was that I never heard him make absolute pronouncements during his sermons. He never said, "You will go to hell if . . ." because this was not a part of his preaching. In fact, I received almost nothing of substance, which left me free to devise my own theology. My beliefs developed from my interpretation of the Bible, personal experience, and general thinking. Thus, I have been open to new ideas, including the concept of spirit possession when it arose in one of my more unusual cases.

Although there has been much pain in my inability to communicate with my father, his flexibility did help me when I stepped out of the boundaries of the "known" in the field of psychiatry. Had he been dogmatic, his beliefs and rules of conduct would have become the standards against which I judged all experience. If an experience of mine seemed to indicate one conclusion and the dogma against which I judged it indicated my conclusion was "impossible," I might have blinded myself to what could prove to be reality.

Even though my father said little of substance during his sermons, I was always convinced that what he said was the word of God. The minister is a prophet and his words reflect God's way, or so I believed. Since I could not argue with the word of God, I could not disagree with my father or any minister. But I also knew he was very much a human being and I was aware of his numerous weaknesses.

For example, my sister once accidentally left her asthma medication on a table where one of my brothers, little more than a toddler, could reach it. By the time her mistake was discovered, my brother had overdosed and had to be rushed to the hospital.

My family was extremely poor at that time, even though my father had given up his full-time ministerial duties to become an inspector for a manufacturing plant. We never owned a car during those early years and my father relied on his nephew, who lived a good distance away, for all our transportation needs. So he turned to this man for a ride to the hospital rather than rushing out to one of our close neighbors who undoubtedly would have helped in the emergency. As a result, at least twenty minutes was wasted before my brother could get help and by then it was too late. My brother died in convulsions in the hospital's Emergency Room.

My father felt it was his place to preach the funeral service himself. It was extremely difficult for him and I am proud that he had the courage to do something he believed was right. At the same time, my respect for my father was diminished by the knowledge that he possibly could have prevented my brother's death. It was possible that damage caused immediately after the pills were swallowed would have been enough to take my brother's life regardless of what was done. But I didn't know that for certain. All I knew was that he got to the hospital twenty minutes later than necessary. Had my father been flexible enough to deviate from his normal routine, my brother would have had professional help much sooner.

What bothered me most, I suppose, was my father's complete lack of guilt. He simply was not aware that he could have done anything differently. In his eyes he had done everything possible. He was seemingly incapable of considering any other option than the one he took, both at the time of the crisis and upon later reflection. It was indeed a paradox since he seemed to abhor such rigidity in his religious work.

Although I was probably justified in my criticism of my father, I have had to face the fact that I too failed my little brother. I was fifteen, old enough to be aware of an alternative to calling my cousin, yet I said nothing. I could have told father to call a neighbor, or called for help myself. Instead, I let him handle everything without ever mentioning a solution which was so obvious to me. It was my failure, as much as my father's inability to see alternatives, that killed my brother.

I know this guilt is a major reason why I have gotten so involved with my patients. Even when their lives were not immediately threatened, I have neglected family, friends, and pleasurable pursuits to answer what, to the patient at least, was an emergency call. I have made house visits when I thought them appropriate and taken telephone calls in the late hours of the night. The tension and the stress of this kind of life have strained family relations and given me a bleeding ulcer. But I am determined never again to be an idle viewer in the midst of crisis. If my brother's death weakened my father's image in my eyes, it also glaringly revealed my own lack of self-worth as I perceived it.

I was already thinking of a possible career at the time of my brother's death. I looked upon my father as a failure in the ministry and had no intention of following in his footsteps. At the same time, I had a tremendous desire to do the kind of work that is beneficial to others. That was when I considered medicine and, more specifically, pediatrics, so I could save other little boys who got into trouble as my brother had. I had let one child die. Through medicine I would help other children experience a better life.

Feeling very noble, I declared myself interested in pediatrics when I went to medical school. Unfortunately, the harsh realities of the medical world quickly changed my plans. The babies and small children were a delight and I could easily tend to their needs. Mothers, on the other hand, were difficult to handle. Perhaps I had not developed adequate compassion at that point, and the endless hours of work may have left me so tired and strained that I took an extreme viewpoint. In any case, I found myself emotionally drained from dealing with worried mothers. I dropped my plans for a pediatric specialty.

Later I learned that I wasn't the only one who had difficulty dealing with my father, although his other problems stemmed from his temper rather than his approach to religion. Because my father was so withdrawn from others, he did not express his concern or irritation with minor daily problems. When something irritated him, he didn't attempt to deal with it in an appropriate manner at the time it occurred. Instead, he held it inside, compounding the tension with each new stress until he absolutely had to let loose. Then he exploded in a rage totally inappropriate to the triggering irritation, at least as far as anyone could tell. They didn't realize that his extreme reaction to a minor incident was a result of the pressures felt from a number of different events, all unrelated. Even if they had, it is doubtful that such behavior would have been tolerated.

My family constantly moved from community to community and church to church as I grew older. Eventually there were no more church positions and my father had to take a job in a manufacturing plant, preaching occasionally on Sundays as a guest minister. My mother always managed to make each new church seem like a joyous calling. I did not learn until much later that the moves were a direct result of my father's inability to get along with the various congregations. He apparently lost his temper once too often in each area, and he was forced to move on because the congregations would not tolerate his explosions.

The ministry does not pay high salaries and I always had to help the family by working at part-time jobs while in school. During the summer before my junior and senior years in high school I was weighing career choices rather seriously.

Then I met a girl who had just been hired where I worked. She was quite attractive and we often talked together. One day she took my hands while we were discussing careers. She studied them for a few moments, then said, "You ought to go into medicine. You have the hands of a doctor." I didn't have the slightest idea what a doctor's hands looked like, but I enjoyed our physical contact too much to insult her by saying so. However, her comment coincided with my own thoughts about medicine since my brother's death, and it began to seem like a logical field for me. I had to promise to become a medical missionary when I applied for a Presbyterian church educational scholarship in order to pay for college. Otherwise the money would have to be paid back. Apparently I showed an unusual amount of zeal because my father, who sat with the panel, said I gave the impression that my concept of medical missionary work was to "go out, cut open people's stomachs, and stuff religion inside."

In any case, I entered medicine with much dedication, but little real knowledge. I was completely unprepared for what I would find.

Anybody who enters the medical field immediately understands why doctors refer to the profession as a practice, not a science. Only so much book learning is possible, and even this body of knowledge changes every few years as old concepts are gradually discarded and new theories accepted. A good part of any doctor's training involves putting textbook knowledge into actual practice, and a small number of patients may die because of a new doctor's ineptitude. Of all people, I know that only too well. I was at least partially responsible for the loss of more than one patient during my training.

While I was an intern in Oakland's Highland Hospital, a man who had been attacked by a burglar was brought in. The burglar had struck him on the head, knocking him out. He was found several hours later and rushed to the Emergency Room. He became one of the number of patients for whom I was responsible that night.

At around three in the morning I was called to the patient's room. He was having great difficulty breathing and his face was turning blue. I could tell that conventional treatment wouldn't save him. He needed an emergency procedure known as a tracheotomy.

Basically, in a tracheotomy the doctor cuts a hole in the trachea, or windpipe, by slicing directly through the skin. Air comes through the neck to the trachea, by-passing the obstruction that is preventing the patient from breathing.

I looked at the patient and desperately thought back to my training. We had learned about this procedure, but it had only been touched on, not fully explained. I had never done one and had never seen one done. I was terrified that if I cut into his neck and missed his windpipe, I might sever one of the arteries, causing him to bleed to death. Yet he was dying before my eyes. Theoretically, I knew what to do but I couldn't summon the courage to plunge a scalpel into his throat because I was afraid my inexperienced hand would compound the problem. In my panic I failed to realize that doing nothing for him was more dangerous than a poorly done tracheotomy.

I rushed from the patient's room and raced down the hall to find the surgical resident. He had worked in the hospital longer than I had and was fully trained in the skills needed to open the patient's windpipe successfully. Where I might blunder with the scalpel, he would use one deft, perfect stroke to expose the needed air passage.

The surgical resident ran back to the patient's room with

me. He grabbed a sterile pack of instruments and was about to open it when we reached the patient's side. The man was dead. My panic run to get help had cost him his life. I had failed to do the job I had been trained for during all the long hours of college and medical school. My name tag said that I was a doctor but at that moment I was convinced I was morally as reprehensible as a cold-blooded hit-man. I didn't know then whether I could have saved that patient by trying the tracheotomy myself. I also had had no idea when I left him how long that patient could live. But I did know that, as it turned out, my failure to try the procedure had eliminated the patient's one chance.

My face was white as I left the room with the surgical resident. My stomach was churning and I was afraid that I would vomit. My eyes stung as I forced back the tears. I needed to talk about what had happened and the role I had played. I needed to expose and explore my feelings with the resident, who was more experienced in both medicine and facing death than I was. Unfortunately, if that other doctor was aware of my inner turmoil, he gave no indication. He walked away from me and returned to whatever he had been doing. The same was true of the other staff members who learned of the death either that night or the next day. No one said anything to me. No one offered me words of advice and even the opportunity to express my feelings. It was as though the dead man was just another statistic, unimportant to anyone, and certainly not a reason for emotional trauma on my part. Undoubtedly, this wasn't their real attitude. I like to think that medicine attracts the strongly compassionate, and that my colleagues' seeming coldness was a defense mechanism to prevent them from becoming so emotionally involved that they couldn't function. Yet I felt hostility about their reaction at the time.

I had to live with that death for many months. It was a periodic part of my dreams and I frequently thought about it when working with other emergency patients under my care. In time I adjusted to the fact that I had been at least partially responsible and could not change that. I could never return the dead to life. From that day forward I tried to educate myself as fully as possible so I would never again inadvertently be responsible for someone's death.

Even when my training was over, I had fears to conquer. I remember how scared and unsure I was when I first went into private practice. While a doctor is in training, there is always someone around to review his or her work. If I was unsure of a treatment step, a senior student or one of the professors was always there to discuss the problem with me. I used my best judgment, which was either reinforced or changed by those around me. It was a very comfortable feeling because I never had a sense of total responsibility. I did not have to risk the feelings I had experienced when I failed to perform the tracheotomy on the emergency patient.

The patients didn't help to bolster my confidence in those early days on my own. They looked upon me as all-knowing, all-wise, and fully capable of helping them through even the most complex problems, despite the fact that I was still learning. A patient might relate the most horrible story of psychological abnormalities I had ever encountered, then turn to me, smiling, and say, "But of course you understand all that, Doctor. Now what can I do about it?"

Perhaps I did understand about it. Certainly they weren't bringing me anything I hadn't studied in the textbook or lectures. But that was the problem; my understanding was intellectual. I had never known a real, living, breathing human being who had had such an experience. To a degree it was embarrassing. And I knew that whatever I said might affect the person's life for years to come. I had what amounted to a kind of power over my patients, and I did not like the idea of that kind of control. At the same time, I wanted to help and knew that my knowledge might truly work for the patient. I had to try, no matter how uncertain I might be.

I began making suggestions that I knew were at least theoretically correct, yet I couldn't escape the feeling that I was experimenting with the patient. If I discovered the theory I applied was practical through the experience of the patient, then I would apply it with confidence the next time around. But there was always a chance the theory might not be applicable to the real situation and I didn't have the slightest idea what I would do if that proved to be the case.

My attempts to solve the problem of my inexperience led to my obsession with psychiatry. I devoted all my waking hours to a mastery of the field. I was determined to gain some of the all-encompassing knowledge patients seemed to think I had. I saw patients and studied the literature of the field eight hours a day and four hours every evening throughout the week. On Saturdays I worked another eight hours. Then on Sunday I caught up with my billing and paper work. Occasionally there was time to say hello to my wife and get reacquainted with the children.

I wasn't deliberately neglecting my family. I was trying to become worthy of the trust my patients had in me. However, this did not lessen the strain on my family and home life.

In those early years, I also had to develop an office "style." Many psychiatrists believe they must find hidden meanings in everything. My wife used to complain about some of my colleagues to whom a simple good-morning was an invitation to elaborate analysis.

I agreed with her and tried to avoid playing the same game. I believed that if people came to a psychiatrist with their problems, they probably saw the doctor as their last resort. I saw no reason to assume that they would hold back either facts or feelings. Of course, some patients could not or would not reveal all their problems, but I felt that most said exactly what they meant while they were in my office, although their perspective was generally not as objective as my own. I tried to avoid searching for hidden meanings when the expressed problem was obviously the true difficulty. I tried to avoid twisting and turning every word I heard in order to create a half dozen problems which probably didn't even exist. I tried to be as straight with my patients as possible since it's often too easy for a psychiatrist to exercise too much control—and power—in a doctor-patient relationship.

Psychiatrists do exercise a great deal of power in our society. Not only do we influence patients, we also can control their freedom.

In those early days of practice, I would frequently be hired to give my professional opinion about people who were in the court system. An alcoholic was arrested repeatedly for actions he took while drunk, for example. The judge sent him to me for evaluation. After I talked with him, I had to let the judge know whether or not I thought the person would repeat his antisocial actions. If I thought his behavior pattern would continue unless he had help, I was supposed to recommend that he be committed to the state hospital for at least ninety days. He would have no choice in the matter, so, in effect, such an action really meant his imprisonment. He wouldn't be in jail, but his freedom of movement would be equally restricted.

Of course, the basic issue is how many chances someone should have before being forced into professional treatment. I was one of the professionals who made that kind of determination and it was rare that the judge disagreed. This power meant that my opinions had tremendous weight and that was very unsettling. I did not feel that any man, especially one as inexperienced as I was then, should have such absolute power. At the same time, I was unable to find a better approach, and I could only hope that my judgment was correct.

Fortunately, psychiatrists seldom have to face serious consequences for their decisions. The people who are committed in this way are usually helped and, at worst, are deprived of their freedom for a relatively short period of time. Yet all too often psychiatrists begin to believe that their opinions are special and that they have unusual insight into people beyond the realities of their training. They become overconfident and a tragedy occurs. I know this only too well, for, as you will see, I would one day make that mistake as well, a mistake which contributed to the suicide of someone I desperately wanted to live.

Chapter 2

Janette, Who Chose to Live

There are moments in life that are so momentous that they forever affect the course of your future existence. The first physical stirrings of puberty mark the end of childhood and the start of a process that leads to independence and adulthood. The rite of marriage ceremoniously announces that you have chosen to share your life with another person. A first job, the birth of a child, a new home are all easily recognized steps marking major life changes.

But the day my personal and professional life changed forever was so unexceptional that I failed to recognize it at the time. It was an ordinary day in March of 1972 and the patient whose illness would trigger the change seemed no different than hundreds of others I had treated.

Janette and her husband were fairly new to Santa Cruz, having previously lived in Oklahoma and Arizona. They came to my office quite by chance, having previously seen another psychiatrist in the community. The psychiatrist had been skilled and reputable, but Janette had had a personality clash with him and knew she could not continue treatment. If a patient cannot work effectively with a particular doctor, he or she should be referred elsewhere. Every psychiatrist has had this experience at one time or another.

Janette sat quietly in my office, her hands folded in her lap, her head down, her long, rather stringy hair hanging limply. She was obviously severely depressed but otherwise seemed like an ordinary housewife.

The brief medical history I took that first day was not particularly unusual, although it was obvious that Janette had been having psychological problems for quite some time. She was twenty-nine years old and her troubles seemed to date back to the seventh grade when she began doing poorly in school. She barely passed her courses each year, and she dropped out in her sophomore year of high school to take a job as a waitress in the Oklahoma city where she lived.

Janette lived at home while she worked as a waitress, a situation she found increasingly intolerable. She became so depressed because of her mother, whom she described as a bossy hypochondriac, always whining about imagined ailments, that she took an overdose of aspirin at age fifteen. She was hospitalized, then returned home.

When Janette was seventeen, she married a man she had been dating for three months just to get out of the house. Unfortunately, neither one loved the other. She was his "proof of normality"—in reality, he was a homosexual who was unable to come to terms with his sexual preference. The marriage was obviously unpleasant from the start and Janette had to be hospitalized twice for depression before she had the sense to divorce the man.

During this first marriage, which lasted five years, Janette and her husband moved to Arizona, and it was there that she was hospitalized. Among other treatments, she was given electroshock therapy, a long-used technique of applying weak current to the two sides of the head in order to cause convulsions and unconsciousness. No one knows exactly what happens during this experience, but severely depressed patients frequently feel better about themselves afterward.

Part of Janette's depression was perfectly understandable. She had had a baby by her first husband and, as happens occasionally, the umbilical cord became twisted about his neck during birth. The infant was deprived of oxygen for a crucial few moments and was born retarded. Her husband irrationally blamed her, insisting there was something wrong with a wife who would "allow" such a terrible accident to occur. Janette accepted responsibility even though she certainly had nothing at all to do with the birth injury. Feeling depressed under such circumstances would be normal for anyone.

Janette's second husband, Lee, was also one of life's losers. He was a skilled mechanic but he had spent most of his time drifting from area to area. When he was out of work, he would go to a bar and challenge any taker to a fight. Bets would be collected from the patrons, then Lee would go outside to prove his skills as a brawler. He never lost and, as a result, always managed to get by financially.

Janette met Lee in a bar and they were drawn to each other immediately. Both were lonely and troubled, yet they felt that together they might make something of themselves. They got married, and Janette had another child. However, the marriage wasn't a success. Lee had the urge to roam and was never comfortable with a steady job. Janette continued to have periods of depression and seemed unable to find happiness with the man she loved and who obviously adored her as well. They stayed married for six years, got a divorce, then decided they couldn't stand living apart. They moved to Santa Cruz and remarried. I met them four months later.

We began talking about the problems that had brought Janette to my office. She said she was compulsive. Some mornings she got up early, began cleaning the house, and was not able to stop. At other times she became depressed and was unable to accomplish anything. She felt hostile toward Lee and thought about killing him. Even worse, she had fantasies about killing her children. For two or three weeks she had suffered from occasional nausea and vomiting but otherwise felt normal physically. She said that she had taken LSD and also used too much alcohol at times.

The last hospital in which Janette had been treated had diagnosed her problems as a form of schizophrenia. I questioned that diagnosis, however, because Janette had failed to respond to any of the medications used to help schizophrenics. It had always been my experience that when medication fails to alter the condition labeled schizophrenia, a different illness, although somewhat similar in symptoms, is the actual culprit.

There are three mental illnesses that people tend to confuse with one another, although they actually have little in common. These disorders are schizophrenia, manic-depression, and multiple personality. The exact nature of each ailment will vary with the individual, but they are always distinctly different from one another.

Most of us casually call schizophrenia "split personality," implying that the sufferer acts like two different people. However, this is not accurate. Imagine instead that all humans have three layers: thoughts form the first layer, emotions form another layer, physical reactions make up the third layer.

In a normal person, these three layers are properly symmetrical. You become aware of something, such as the death of your grandmother, then have an emotional and physical reaction to the news. The intellectual awareness of the event, in this case a death, is identical in both the normal and the schizophrenic individual. However, while the normal person will then grieve, the schizophrenic may have an entirely different emotional response. He or she may laugh, finding the tragic news humorous. Or he or she may not respond at all. A schizophrenic's emotional responses are inappropriate for the reality of the situation.

What makes the schizophrenic unique is that this type of emotional short-circuiting continues throughout the person's life. It doesn't happen once a week or once a month. The person exhibits irrational behavior every day.

It is now believed that schizophrenia is a genetically determined condition. The tendency toward it is inherited and it is probably the result of a biochemical defect in the brain. Although this is still only theory, it is possible to control the disease with drugs called phenothiazines. Patients are not cured, but with continuing medication they can lead a normal life.

Janette told me she heard voices upon occasion, but the phenothiazine she had been given did not alter this problem. She was also aware that such voices were not normal and she was concerned about what it all meant. A true schizophrenic would have accepted the voices as real, without thinking that he or she had a problem.

The chemical imbalance that apparently causes schizophrenia also results in a body odor that people who work around mentally disturbed patients can spot. I have heard many attendants and nurses in mental hospitals tell me they can identify schizophrenics by their smell. It is neither strong nor offensive, but it is different enough to be obvious.

Manic-depressives also have a hereditary problem, but their body chemistry differs so their response to life is different. In manic-depression, the mental defect is exhibited in the extremes of mood control. Moods swing from high to low. The person's thoughts will center on joyous experiences or morbid ideas, depending upon these moods. Some people alternate between normality and manic behavior while others alternate between normality and depression. However, most sufferers swing from extreme highs to extreme lows with a normal period halfway through the cycle. These shifts in mood are totally unrelated to the external events that would affect a normal person.

Diagnosis of manic-depression can be difficult because patients with other mental illnesses often exhibit many of the symptoms found in the manic phase. Patients in this phase are euphoric, convinced that they are the greatest people on earth. Fortunately, a person using an unwarranted sense of greatness as a defense mechanism usually reveals himself by fighting therapy. He doesn't want to see himself objectively and will resist treatment.

A true manic-depressive, on the other hand, has nothing to hide. He or she genuinely feels like the ruler of the world at times and is not trying to repress an inferiority complex or anything else. The patient is extremely cooperative and, as further proof, the individual will exhibit the "down" phases of this illness as well. Thus, the possibility of misdiagnosis is not as great as it would seem.

Lithium is the drug that alters the chemical imbalance of the true manic-depressive. It brings stability to the manic-depressive's existence. It allows the patient to function on an even emotional plane without impairing his or her powers of reasoning or creativity.

Lithium and phenothiazines affect the chemical balance of

the body very differently. Janette had shown inappropriate mood reactions symptomatic of either manic-depression or schizophrenia. Since the phenothiazines failed to work, it was fairly certain that manic-depression was the more appropriate diagnosis. I decided to prescribe lithium for her, along with other medication, and made another appointment for her.

A few days later Janette returned to my office. She was more neatly groomed; her hair was fixed, her eyebrows plucked and penciled. But she seemed withdrawn. She responded to my questions with as few words as possible. She seemed unhappy with her family but would not go into enough detail for me to determine if the problem went beyond the manic-depressive state. Since she seemed more depressed than she had on the previous visit, I assumed she was in that phase of the illness and, with luck, the continued use of the lithium would level her off and allow her to function normally. I ran the tests necessary to be certain she had an adequate, safe dose of lithium, then sent her home. Nothing seemed out of the ordinary.

Had I had any hint of a problem, I would have hospitalized Janette immediately. However, I thought her emotions would be controlled by the lithium, so I was shocked when Lee called to tell me she had been hospitalized after attempting suicide.

In theory, a doctor should be constantly alert to the possibility of suicide. In reality, many psychiatrists try to deny or minimize the suicidal tendencies of some of their patients. If we were forced to acknowledge the gravity of the problem, we might have to demand that some patients be forced into the hospital for a seventy-two-hour observation period against their will. We don't want to rouse the ire of the patients or their families, so we tend to put our own convenience ahead of what should be obvious signals.

When patients talk of suicide, we sometimes tell ourselves that as long as they just talk about it, they are not actually going to do it. Yet statistically we know this isn't true. If they talk of killing themselves, chances are they will try to do just that.

Later in my career I became active in suicide prevention organizations, initiating hot lines and similar services. I learned ways to recognize a potential suicide and prevent the person from acting on the suicidal impulse. For example, I would make a "contract" with the patient whereby the patient would agree to wait to kill himself or herself until after seeing me. It was an attainable goal for the patient. He or she didn't feel the need to prove anything by dying immediately. The person retained the option of suicide but put it off for several hours or several days. If you can delay suicide long enough, the person eventually learns to cope through intensive therapy, without taking drastic, self-destructive action.

Janette, however, took me by surprise with her attempt. I didn't know whether I had lied to myself about the danger signals or if, for some strange reason, there had been no advance warning. I only knew that I was caught unaware when she made the attempt and I thanked God that she had failed. I also began questioning my own abilities, since I too had failed, and my failure was far more serious. I felt that somehow I could have prevented her attempt.

As soon as Janette was out of physical danger, I placed her in the psychiatric ward. I then asked a psychologist I knew to conduct various tests to help me determine what problems she might have other than manic-depressive illness. The psychologist was highly skilled and I trusted her opinion. Her involvement saved me a great deal of time that I could devote to counseling other patients currently in treatment.

The next evening I was in bed when the telephone rang. It was late and I was surprised to hear the psychologist's voice. Normally she called me in my office. I was worried that Janette had made a second attempt on her life and the anxiety in the psychologist's voice added to my alarm.

"Ralph, do you know what you've got with that patient you asked me to see?"

"No, Katherine," I said. "That's why I asked you to run that battery of psychological tests."

"You've got another *Three Faces of Eve* on your hands."

"What are you talking about? Are you telling me that Janette is a multiple personality? Come off it, Katherine. Do you know how rare those cases are? Nobody ever sees one of them. I mean, I suppose they're out there, but I'm not going to have one walking into my office."

"Ralph, I'm telling you it's a classic case. I went in to see her and she was talking about how she didn't belong in the hospital. She was walking about, rather agitated, saying there was nothing wrong with her. '*She's* the one who's depressed, not me,' she told me. '*She's* the one who's got problems.'

"She was talking in the third person like that and I had the feeling she was talking about Janette. It was like she was somebody else and not the person I was there to see at all, even though, of course, it was the same person. It's a classic example, Ralph. I'm certain that's her problem."

"I'll . . . I'll be in to see her first thing tomorrow," I said, hanging up the telephone.

I was shocked. Katherine wasn't an inexperienced graduate student. She was a trained professional with plenty of experience. I had always been able to trust her conclusions about the cases we had worked on together. If she said that Janette was a multiple personality, then she must have had strong reasons for her conclusion.

But multiple personality?

I tried to remember what little I knew about the subject. We had never discussed it at U.C.L.A., nor had it come up during my psychiatric residency at Stanford Medical Center. In fact, my total exposure to the subject had been little more than going to see Joanne Woodward in *The Three Faces of Eve* when I was serving in the Air Force. My wife and I found the movie interesting and I was able to understand some of the possible causes of multiple personality, but the case was made into a movie primarily because it was so unusual. Eve and her three personalities didn't enter the life of the average psychiatrist. If one such case was reported in my lifetime, I figured that would probably be about it. I was certain that it was a phenomenon that would never involve me as a practicing psychiatrist.

And yet, Katherine, the psychologist, had been so certain. . . .

Throughout the night my thoughts kept returning to Janette's problem and my potential involvement. I tried to view the matter on an intellectual level, thinking about the concept of multiple personality and how I might deal with such a patient. I knew almost nothing about the illness and had never studied it in medical school. Most likely Katherine was mistaken, and if she wasn't, undoubtedly I could find someone else to take Janette's case.

What I denied was the churning sensation in my stomach that indicated my true emotions. I had gas and nausea, sensations I alternately ignored and then ascribed to the dinner I had eaten. I did not want to face the fact that I was scared. I did not want to admit that I was back to the first day in private practice when a patient looked up to me and I had only the slightest idea of what to do next. I wanted older and wiser psychiatrists, men and women with generations of experience, to sit by my side and guide my next meeting with Janette.

Unfortunately, I didn't know any likely candidates and, even if I did, I probably would not have been able to obtain their assistance. I had been in practice long enough to make me the individual new psychiatrists might seek out for assistance. I was supposed to be reasonably learned and totally competent. But I wasn't. I had always tried to do my best, but now I was breaking new ground. I was uneducated in this field, lost, and terrified of my weakness. I prayed that I might do the right thing and wondered if I should turn Janette over to another doctor immediately. Finally, after hours of agonizing and trying to deny my fear, I decided to see Janette and analyze the situation before taking any further action.

I felt alert as I entered the hospital the next morning, despite a sleepless night. I suppose my adrenaline was flowing as I prepared myself for what was to come.

Janette was as I remembered her—quiet, introverted, and depressed. If anything, she was embarrassed by what she had done. "I don't even remember taking all those pills," Janette told me. "There's no reason for me to want to kill myself. My children need me." Her voice was weak and she looked down at the floor as she spoke.

"Janette, the psychologist who saw you yesterday says there's someone else here with you," I began. Somebody should write an etiquette book about how to approach a potential multiple personality. I didn't have the slightest idea what I was doing or what the results might be.

Janette looked puzzled.

"What I mean is, there's someone inside your head—someone else sharing your body."

I suppose another patient might have told me that I was nuttier than the people locked in isolation. But Janette was too meek. However, by the expression on her face, I could tell that she thought I had been drinking too much.

"I want to meet the other person. I think I can if you'll give me a little cooperation. Will you?" She looked puzzled by my request but trusted me enough to go along with it.

"All right, Dr. Allison. What do you want me to do?" she asked.

"Janette, just relax, close your eyes, and listen to my voice. Let whatever will happen, happen. I won't let anything hurt you, believe me."

I wasn't sure what I was going to do. I was so nervous that my voice almost cracked. But it was essential that I sound confident and wise so Janette would relinquish conscious control of her body. I hoped I could call out whomever Katherine had talked to the night before. If there was "someone" inside, that personality apparently was willing to communicate, so there was some reason to hope I was doing the right thing.

After a few minutes of encouragement, Janette relaxed and I said, in a commanding, forceful voice, "Now I want to talk to whoever or whatever spoke to the psychologist last night. Come out by the time I count to three. One . . . Two . . . Three!"

On the count of three, Janette's body stiffened and her previously blank facial expression became hard and calculating. Her eyes opened and she watched me suspiciously. "Okay, doc, what do you want?" said the voice coming from Janette's body. It was harsh, grating, and loud. Her stance was that of a woman who had seen and done so much that nothing could possibly surprise her. "And God, it's good to get rid of that piss-ass Janette."

It was like something out of a movie. It was Joanne Woodward changing from Eve White to Eve Black in *The Three Faces of Eve*. The memory of that movie flashed in my mind. I visualized the meek housewife, Eve White, suddenly becoming the hostile, sexually aggressive Eve Black, who liked to go to the bars in town and pick up sailors. But this wasn't a movie. This wasn't an actress playing a role. This was a living, breathing human whose mind had shattered into fragments, each of which had a unique character.

It was the kind of experience that seemed almost like a fantasy. Janette's tone of voice, mannerisms, and appearance were different. I knew that if I saw this cocky, self-possessed, volatile woman from a distance as she walked down the street, I would never suspect that she and the Janette I knew were the same person. "Then you're not Janette?" I asked, my voice slightly hoarse from surprise.

My nerves were shaken. My heart was racing and I could feel sweat on my forehead. I told myself to treat this as a learning experience. I was seeing something new in my field and I should observe whatever might develop. I shouldn't try to evaluate it or label it. I would watch and wait for her to give me more clues about what was going on inside her head.

The woman smiled and stood up, stretching her arms and legs. Slowly she walked around me, looking me up and down as she passed, apparently trying to decide whether or not I was worth her time. "Do you think I'm that piss-ass?" she said. She moved over to the bed in her room and sat down. Her legs were slightly spread apart and her skirt covered only a portion of her thighs. She looked like a prostitute trying to lure a man into bed.

"You're kinda cute. I bet you know a lot of tricks, being a psychiatrist. How about closing the door and giving me a tumble?"

If the situation hadn't been so serious, it might have been almost humorous. I am what is politely termed a "big" man. I'm well over six feet tall, heavier than I should be, and far from a woman's ideal of a romantic "leading man." Janette was what some people would call a "mouse." Yet she was acting as though I was an ideal sex object. It was ridiculous. Even worse, it confirmed Katherine's opinion that multiple personality might be a factor in this case.

"Who are you?" I said, staying near the door, well away from the woman on the bed. I had no intention of chancing even the slightest hint of impropriety. She kept away from me while she was talking, but if she was serious, I wanted to be able to get out of the room and get help quickly. "Do you have a name?"

"Name? Hell, I guess you can call me Lydia. And the whole trouble with me is that I'm trapped in this piss-ass body and *she* doesn't want to do a damn thing that's fun."

"What do you consider 'fun'?"

"Drinking . . . dancing . . . getting fucked. What else is there in life?" She winked at me, then shifted her body to what I suppose was meant to be a more provocative position.

"When do you do these things?"

"Whenever I can get control of the body. Hell, doc, do you know what it's like being kept a prisoner in Goody Two-Shoes here? I want to break loose every night but I can't do it. I'm getting better, though. I'm getting out, popping pills, picking up men more and more. One day I'm going to kill this bitch. Hell, she doesn't have any idea of how to have fun. If this body's going to get around and enjoy the pleasures in life, I'm the one who's got to take control and do it."

As I listened to the woman in front of me, I was responding to the conversation on two levels. Intellectually, I found the situation fascinating. For years I had been studying the human mind and I had been intrigued by the complexities and ambiguities in human thought and behavior. Now I had the chance to study one of the most unusual types of mental illness anyone could encounter.

Unfortunately, I wasn't studying a textbook. In front of me was a human being who had put her faith in my ability to help her lead a normal life. The complexity of her problem seemed overwhelming, but I decided to act anyway, not knowing what might happen next.

"Is there anyone else in there?" I asked. "Is there someone I haven't met?" I had no idea what my request might bring. I wanted to think that I was dealing with Lydia and Janette, no one else. Two different personalities somehow seemed potentially manageable—no worse than the mood shifts of a manic-depressive patient. Any more would be a nightmare, yet I had come this far and I knew I didn't dare make any assumptions about this case. Because of my inexperience, I had to explore every possibility, no matter how silly or unscientific it might seem at first.

"Come off it, doc. I'm the best piece in California. Why do you want to go elsewhere looking for your kicks?"

My voice became more authoritative. "If there's someone else in there, I want to meet her—now!"

"Doc, lay off," said Lydia, her voice rising as though she was frightened of someone. "I don't get out enough. I don't . . ." Lydia's voice trailed off as her eyes glazed for a moment, then seemed to clear. They were suddenly softer, no longer penetrating. The entire face appeared to relax and the muscles of her body lost their tension.

"Janette? Are you back?"

The woman before me looked intently at my face, then let out a deep sigh. When she spoke, her voice was soft, gentle, and immensely sad. "I'm not Janette," she said. "My name is Marie and I'm so tired of all this. In and out of hospitals so often . . . I've tried to protect her over the years, but it's been so hard and I'm not a strong person—"

"Protect her?"

"From herself . . . From Lydia . . . So many problems, and I just can't seem to find the strength to go on. Sometimes I think it would be so peaceful to just go to sleep and never wake up."

"Are you the one who took the overdose of pills?" There it was, my acceptance of the unacceptable. I was convinced by now that this woman was indeed a multiple-personality sufferer. I accepted each change of personality as the equivalent of talking with a unique woman.

"Yes, I took the pills. I know suicide is wrong but this life has been such a nightmare for everyone. I just didn't see the point in continuing as we were."

"Do you still feel that way?"

"No, it's wrong and I doubt that I could ever find the courage to try again. I'll continue the way I always have, bearing the burdens Janette can't handle and facing the shame of Lydia's actions."

I talked with this new personality a few more minutes,

then asked to speak to Janette. I didn't ask about anyone else inside the body, probably because I was afraid of what I might find. It seemed logical to assume that I had met everyone who might be there, though experience with other such patients now convinces me I was hasty.

Then Marie's stance and attitude changed and Janette reappeared. To my surprise, she had no knowledge of what had gone on while I was talking to Lydia and Marie.

I didn't know how to approach Janette. I didn't even know who or what she was, although I hoped she was the main personality. I liked her, and since she had been the personality who came to see me, I looked upon her as my primary patient. Whatever happened during treatment, I assumed she would be the one who would survive. Yet how could I break the news to her?

"Janette . . ." I began. My voice was none too steady, but I didn't want my nervousness to show. A psychiatrist should be firm, strong, in command of every situation. It helps the patient build confidence in the doctor. That confidence is not always justified, of course, but without it, there is little chance the patient will get better. "The hospitals in which you've been treated said you were schizophrenic, but as we discussed in my office, the diagnosis is probably not correct. You didn't respond to the medication and your thought pattern is normal."

"Yes, Doctor . . ." Her voice was low, almost a whisper. She was the type of person who lived in dread of another person's anger. She was meek, subdued, radically different from Lydia. And yet it was the same person, at least physically.

"After my examination I told you I thought you were suffering from manic-depressive illness. That's why I've been giving you lithium."

"I've been following your advice faithfully, though I'm afraid it's not doing any more for me than the other drugs."

"I know that. And I think I know the reason why."

Janette looked at me intently, her expression one of expectation. She did not like living the way she had been. She was anxious to lead a normal life. I could tell that she wanted me to identify her problems once and for all so that she could finally begin feeling like everyone else.

"Do you remember my saying that there was someone else inside your head? I asked to speak to that person—and I did."

"I don't understand. I don't remember what happened after that. I forget things sometimes. I can't recall the last few minutes, but there's nothing odd about that, is there? Lots of people forget things, don't they?"

"Not like you do, Janette. Not if my suspicions are correct." I then explained what I knew about multiple personality, implying that it was a problem with which I was reasonably well acquainted. I had to instill the desire to get better in Janette.

She seemed to accept my explanation, although I later found that it was only a superficial acceptance. It would be many weeks before she truly recognized how sick she was.

As soon as I left my new patient, I went to the hospital library and began an intensive study of every piece of literature ever published on multiple personality. I read *The Three Faces of Eve,* which was written by two doctors who, I thought, might offer clues to the treatment of such patients. They didn't; nor were the other references very helpful. However, I did begin to acquire a superficial understanding of the illness.

Multiple personality is actually a coping mechanism of the mind. It is a way of handling problems that otherwise seem overwhelming. When the whole individual can't cope, a separate personality is created to handle different emotions. Thus, Lydia was filled with anger and a craving for cheap thrills. Marie, I later learned, professed to be a good Christian woman who had been in charge of the body when the marriage with Lee took place. Pregnancies followed almost immediately, but they were unsuccessful. She carried the couple's first two children, each of whom was born dead. The shock of the loss of the children, which she interpreted as punishment for some sin, greatly upset her and she seldom took control of the body. And Janette was a tense, frigid, puritanical woman who tried to cope with the everyday chores of living.

Multiple personality differs from other forms of mental illness in that the personalities are consistent in everything they do. A schizophrenic is not particularly logical, as has been shown. But each personality of a multiple will act the same way each time he or she comes out.

Little was actually known about multiple personality according to the available literature I searched in my effort to understand Janette. The cases reported were few in number, and most of the observations were of individuals who were seen and studied but never cured. It is only today, after working with more than forty patients, almost all of whom developed normal lives as whole individuals, that I begin to have an understanding of this illness. And I know that there may still be much more to learn.

I have learned, for example, that certain patterns of causation are somewhat consistent. Child abuse is a factor, but this need not be physical brutality. Some patients were brutalized by one or both parents; others received psychological or mental harassment.

The multiple-personality patient generally experiences polarity in family relationships as a child. One parent is seen as being "good" while the other is "bad." However, the roles sometimes change, and the "good" parent does something "bad," which can confuse the child. Often the "good" parent will "abandon" the child through death, military service, or some other normal separation that the child cannot understand.

Frequently, children who develop alter personalities are taught to repress their anger and negative feelings. "Good girls don't get angry," is the attitude conveyed by their parents or guardians. They are also taught to hide family "sins" from the world, which makes psychiatric treatment initially very difficult for them.

Children who become multiple-personality patients are also unusually sensitive to those around them. They retain this extreme sensitivity all their lives, often to the point of having psychic abilities. Henry Hawksworth, one of my former patients, could see auras, for example—colors around people that reflected their moods. Even after his personalities were fused, he retained enough of this special sensitivity to be able to utilize it in his work as a personnel director.

Multiple-personality patients also seem to suffer from a psychological defect. They don't learn from experience the way normal people do. The patient does something, gets punished for it, and then goes out and does it again. The punishment doesn't become part of the learning process, nor do they really understand the cause-and-effect relationship between an action and the ensuing punishment.

For example, one personality repeatedly gets drunk—and is always slightly surprised by the hangover that follows. Cause and effect are not connected. Thus, my job as therapist, in part, is to get the idea of personal responsibility across to the patient.

The multiple-personality patient creates personalities that are limited to only one type of activity. One personality may be serious and capable of handling business matters and other important aspects of living. Another personality might be childlike, enjoying toys and games regardless of his or her age. And a third personality might live only for sex.

Each alter personality of a multiple-personality patient acts consistently in all situations. Thus, the business personality will be dominated by thoughts of work whether at the beach or an amusement park, or even in bed. A fun-loving personality will always act like a child. He or she will make paper airplanes in the office, shoot paper clips, and play any number of other games with the company supplies, even during important meetings. Such a person probably has no interest in sex but might answer the sexual aggressiveness of a partner by running and hiding or starting a pillow fight.

The alter personality who is filled with lust knows no restraints. The personality may try to seduce almost anyone of the opposite sex regardless of the role the person plays in the personality's life. The seduction will often be attempted in front of others and in such a crude manner that the effect would be humorous if the alter personality weren't so serious. This total lack of judgment concerning social situations can greatly embarrass loved ones.

While I was trying to educate myself about multiple-personality illnesses, I also tried to learn more about Janette's past. I wrote to various hospitals where she had been treated, attempting to piece together a more complete medical history. I also wrote to her parents, explaining their daughter's problems and seeking their assistance.

Writing to Janette's parents was a gamble. Parents are frequently a cause of adult emotional difficulties. If the parents' actions are *not* one of the problems, the child's misperceptions of those same actions are frequently to blame. Thus, there was a chance that the information they could provide would prove of little value, which was the case.

At the time I wrote to Janette's parents I didn't understand one critical factor—that parents seem to have been a triggering factor in every case I have seen to date. Both the book and the film version of *The Three Faces of Eve,* indicated that the problem had its origins in Eve's childhood, although the book never clarified whether this was parental influence or some unrelated trauma. In any case, I felt that if there was a chance that Janette's family could add information I lacked, it was important that I obtain it.

While waiting for the medical information, I recognized that I was totally inadequate to treat Janette and her alter personalities. I decided to seek help from a friend who ran a large psychiatric ward in a major hospital outside of Santa Cruz. My friend told me that the staff had seen a number of multiple-personality cases and knew how to care for them. If I thought it was advisable to send Janette to his psychiatric facility, he and the staff would treat her.

That was a relief! I was not foolish enough to want to pioneer in little-known areas of psychiatry when there were experienced people in the field to whom I could send my patients. I gathered all the medical information I had on Janette and sent her off to the hospital.

Janette was in the hospital for a total of six weeks before the staff sent her home, pronouncing her "cured." During the early days, both Janette and Lydia had been in control of the body. Janette might go to a group therapy session, for example, sit quietly, and listen to the others relate their problems. Then, without warning, Lydia would take control, taunting the other patients, making obscene suggestions to the men, and generally raising hell. Janette had no memory of these events but accepted the descriptions of the staff and other patients.

The hospital staff felt that the best way to treat Janette was to work with her individually. Whenever Lydia went on one of her rampages, the staff ignored her. They wouldn't talk to her or answer her questions. They ignored her sexual advances and turned a deaf ear to her abusive language.

Gradually, Lydia put in fewer appearances. Finally, several weeks into the treatment, a note in Lydia's handwriting was found, which said, "I quit! I quit! I quit!"

The hospital staff was jubilant. They knew the note meant Lydia was banished forever. When they told me what had happened, I agreed with their conclusion. Several days later Janette was released.

I looked forward to Janette's next visit to my office. I expected to see a basically sound individual whose remaining problems could be solved with normal treatment.

My attitude seems naïve today. Multiple-personality illness is a complex one that often takes months or years of care. But I did not know the realities at that time. I had no understanding of the root causes of multiple personality, so there was no way for me to evaluate the treatment. Eve's consultation with her psychiatrist had lasted for months. However, it was also the psychiatrist's first experience with the problem. I knew that many weeks or months could be wasted as a result of the doctor's lack of knowledge. My friend at the hospital had convinced me that the staff had full understanding of the problem. So I assumed that when Janette was pronounced "cured," she truly was. I could relax, secure in the knowledge that my future would be no different than I had anticipated when I first opened my office.

"You son of a bitch!" roared the woman in front of me. She wore tightly fitted clothes and her blouse was partially unbuttoned. "What sort of place did you send her to, anyway? Do you know what those bastards did? They ignored me! They ignored *ME!* Even the men. Hell, I may not be the best piece of ass that ever walked down the road, but I've got far more going for me than either the nurses or the sickies. And not one of those mothers tried to fuck me!"

Lydia was back.

It was a moment of personal crisis. I was faced with a patient seeking help for a problem that was quite possibly beyond my ability to solve. The sensible thing would have been to refer her elsewhere, but that is precisely what I had done when I sent her to the hospital. The staff members were supposedly experts and *they* had failed to understand that Janette was really leaving the hospital as sick as she had been when she arrived.

Theoretically, I could have turned to the psychiatric literature and looked up the names of doctors who had successfully treated such people. But I had looked over the literature and it was obvious that other doctors didn't really know what they were doing. The Eve White/Eve Black/Jane story in *The Three Faces of Eve* ends with the psychiatrist's admission that Jane seemed to be disintegrating. A doctor either cures a patient or he doesn't. The disintegration of Jane implied that she still needed more treatment or a different kind of treatment, which eventually proved to be the case. Other doctors had merely been observers of patients who had never changed. Still others seemed very much like my friend at the hospital, who ignored the problem and created a "cure" by frustrating, not eliminating, a patient's alter personality.

I knew that I might blunder in my treatment and perhaps fail, yet I resolved to do my best to try to help Janette. I knew that I could do no worse than anyone else, and I did want her to get well.

Looking back, I still wonder if I made the right decision at that stage in my professional development. Was I actually enticed by the idea of blazing new trails in my field? Or, perhaps, was I looking upon Janette as a guinea pig in an intellectual exercise? Or did I simply care about this troubled woman and want to help her get well?

I don't know the answer. I'm not even certain I want to face the reality of my motivations at that time. What is important is that I did plunge forward, disregarding my inexperience and lack of information.

My first step in treating Janette was to try to learn what had happened in the hospital. I mentioned the note Lydia had written, adding, "I figured you had gone back to whatever part of the mind you came from and I would only see Janette."

"Of course I wrote that note," Lydia said. "I wanted those bastards to know I was through with them. If they weren't going to be decent enough to even give me the time of day, why should I stay around there? I let that piss-ass have the body the whole time. Hell, I saw through their game. I knew that if I wanted to get out of there, it was best to keep hidden until they decided little Goody Two-Shoes could go."

I began treatment by playing tape recordings of Lydia and Marie for Janette's benefit. She had no knowledge of either personality and needed the shock of the recordings to convince her more fully of my diagnosis.

I had hoped that my inquiries concerning Janette's background would help. Unfortunately, the hospital records proved of little value since they added nothing new to the information I already had. The letter from her mother told me how terrible Lee was and accused him of sending love letters to a woman in Oklahoma whom he had dated before his marriage. Both parents were aware that their daughter had problems and were most concerned. But I learned almost nothing of value for treatment.

Perhaps the most important step I took in Janette's treatment was the utilization of hypnosis in the hope that it would provide a better understanding of why alter personalities had been created in the first place. I had been studying hypnosis since I first entered practice but this was one of the first times I had utilized it with one of my patients.

There are many misconceptions about hypnosis. One of the most prevalent is the belief that the hypnotizer can dominate the will of his subject. Actually, hypnosis is at least as old as recorded history and many people practice self-hypnosis without realizing it.

Hypnosis simply means that the mind is more open to suggestion than usual. It is similar to the state you are in just before going to sleep. As a result, certain reflex actions that cannot take place during actual sleep are easily visible during the hypnotic state.

The subject's imagination can be stimulated far more readily than in the normal waking state. There is a heightened awareness, and it is possible to break through to the subconscious mind. Thus, experiences that have been repressed and kept out of our conscious awareness can be remembered under hypnosis.

Hypnosis is a perfectly safe therapeutic tool, and even bringing someone out of a trance is quite simple. You can tell them to wake up, snap your fingers, or use any kind of movement or sound. If you leave the room without deliberately awakening your subjects, they will come out of it themselves. However, if left to their own devices, subjects are so relaxed that they often fall into a natural sleep.

Although the psychiatrist using hypnosis can influence the subject's thinking through suggestion, the subject cannot be made to do something he wouldn't do normally. The subject's conscience and normal value system remain unaffected. A righteous individual, for example, cannot be hypnotized into committing a crime.

There are three stages of hypnosis: the lethargic state, the cataleptic state, and the somnambulistic state.

Each represents a somewhat deeper trance. The lightest state, the lethargic one, is a mild trance state in which the person regularly remembers everything that is said and done. Breathing is similar to that of normal sleep and the subject can easily open his or her eyes, although most subjects seldom bother trying.

The hypnotic effect intensifies in the next two stages. The person becomes insensitive to pain and can make his or her limbs rigid. Eventually, the subject becomes completely immobile, moving only when directed to do so. Memory is also impaired during this period. The cataleptic subject retains partial memory of the trance state; the somnambulistic subject loses all memory. In the latter stage memory is retained in the subconscious and can only be triggered by hypnotic suggestion.

Through the use of hypnosis it is possible to take a person back in time to recall events that occurred many years earlier. Sometimes the subject actually relives these events, going through the motions of opening presents on a fifth birthday, for example. At other times the subject is a witness, not a participant of the scene, describing events in a detached manner. A woman might "witness" a rape she experienced as a teen-ager, watching her body being abused as though she were standing nearby rather than being the actual victim of the event.

My first hypnotic efforts with Janette were meant to help

her focus on the reasons for the existence of her alter personalities. I quickly learned that Lydia served to express anger because Janette could not. If Lee did something Janette didn't like, she said nothing. Resentment built up inside but went unexpressed. Eventually the internal pressure was too great and Lydia would take control, going on a violent rampage totally out of proportion to the incident which had initially sparked the feelings of hostility.

Lydia also had fun. Janette had made her home her whole life, even though this was boring and emotionally unhealthy. Lydia, on the other hand, liked places where there was music, drinks, and men out for a good time. Her lifestyle was distinctly opposite that of Janette's.

As I talked with Janette's personalities, a possible treatment approach took shape in my mind. I recognized that Janette had used the multiple personalities as a coping mechanism. If there was something she felt she had to do yet couldn't handle for some reason, the alter personality would take charge without regard for the consequences.

I decided on two simultaneous courses of action. I had to find out what early traumas Janette had experienced. Only then could I help her find coping mechanisms other than mentally splitting into several personalities. Secondly, I had to help Janette do those perfectly normal things the alter personalities were handling. I encouraged her to express the completely normal anger she felt from time to time. When something upset her, she had to force herself to talk about it. She also had to get out of the house and do something she found enjoyable. Only in this way could she lessen her dependence on Lydia.

I was using logic in my treatment because I didn't know what else to do. Even the strangest of mental disorders will have a readily understandable original cause. Sometimes, as in the case of schizophrenia, it is a hereditary problem of body chemistry. In some multiple-personality cases, serious abuse is a major factor.

In Janette's case, it was obvious that she did not feel she dared enjoy herself, so she suppressed this desire, creating an alter personality who could have the fun. If her values and thought processes were strengthened and encouraged, the need for an alter personality would diminish and a cure would be possible.

Lee asked to be a part of the therapy sessions and I was glad to have him. He had problems of his own, but he genuinely cared about his wife and wanted to help her. He encouraged her to speak up when he did something she found upsetting. He told her he would not leave her if she argued with him. He said he would like her more because he could learn how to modify his behavior to keep her happy.

I asked Janette to choose one activity that would truly make her happy. Her life had been confined to such a narrow area that her idea of "breaking loose" was very modest. She wanted to join the P.T.A. and go to their functions with the other mothers. She had two small children in school and knew she was eligible to join.

Janette followed my suggestions diligently. She began telling Lee when she was upset and eventually gained the courage to express irritation toward others when such an emotion was appropriate. She also went to a P.T.A. meeting and came home exhilarated. For her, the P.T.A. was the most enjoyable activity she had ever known.

I had not talked to Lydia for a while so I called her out several sessions after Janette began "letting loose" in her own rather mild way. A different Lydia stood before me. She was still the same worldly-wise individual, but the fight seemed to have left her body. She said she was weakened and I believed it. She complained that she had no energy for sex, drinking, or even taking over the body very often. It was only with almost superhuman effort that she managed to go to the beach one weekend, and once there, she had strength only to sit and wink at the men. Seduction and sex were impossible.

I was delighted. I had hoped that if Janette began taking over activities previously handled by her alter personalities, they would lose their reason for existing and fade into oblivion. But my idea was only a theory and I was unsure of its ability to succeed.

At this point in the treatment I was beginning to feel rather good about myself. I delight in intellectual challenges and there was a tremendous feeling of triumph associated with watching Janette seemingly begin reintegrating her personalities. I had read the literature about one of the most rarely reported mental illnesses, discovering little of value. Then I had analyzed what was reported, mentally comparing it with what I had learned both in school and in private practice. Finally, I developed a treatment approach that was unlike anything that had ever been tried, as far as I knew. It was a fascinating mental puzzle that I appeared to be solving.

To say that I was naïve when I treated Janette would be an understatement. I thought she had fully accepted the multiple-personality diagnosis. Her conversation seemed to indicate that she was comfortable with the diagnosis. She worked with me in therapy and was quite willing to help me with a new patient, named Carrie, who appeared to share Janette's unusual problem.

The truth, however, was quite different from the apparent reality. Janette had never developed a "gut" reaction to the diagnosis, which, I later learned, is necessary to give the patient the will to fight the illness. Before that "gut" acceptance occurs, the patient lacks the drive to become whole. Until then, therapy is more of a game and isn't taken seriously.

Janette's "gut," emotional acceptance came during a therapy session in my office. I had decided to deviate from my normal treatment plan that day. Admittedly, my care of Janette had always been unstructured. My inexperience resulted in a great deal of trial and error. But Janette seemed to be gaining self-awareness, and her need for the multiple-personality coping mechanism was rapidly diminishing.

I maintained only one rigid "rule" during treatment. Whoever brought the "body" to my office also took it home. Thus, if Janette kept the appointment and I asked to talk to Marie, I would recall Janette at the end of the session. This particular day, however, I spent most of the hour talking to Lydia, whom I found to be most unpleasant. When she was ready to leave I let her go, too tired to spend the next few minutes convincing her to let me put her "under" so that Janette could regain control of the body.

Lydia left my office looking for action. I later learned that she picked up two hitchhikers she found along the road. This was something Janette would never have done.

The hitchhikers were two of the raunchiest-looking males imaginable, I was later told. They had long hair that had not been washed in weeks. Their clothing was old, soiled, and smelled of a combination of urine and whiskey. They were so spaced-out on drugs and alcohol that they passed out as soon as they got into the car.

Lydia, who assumed the men might be fun, was disappointed in them when they lost consciousness. She returned control of the body to Janette, whose last memory was of coming to my office.

I knew there was a chance that Janette would take control of the body while Lydia was driving, but I also knew that there was no danger to other motorists. This is one of the remarkable aspects of multiple-personality patients. Because their lives are filled with events you and I would consider strange, they have learned to accept the unacceptable. Janette frequently found herself driving or walking in strange areas and remained in perfect control. A passer-by watching her car would not detect the "change" in drivers as she slipped from one personality to another. Nor was the multiple personality shocked in any way.

As I suspected, the discovery that she was driving down the highway caused only mild surprise, and Janette never lost control of the vehicle. However, when she turned her head to see what was causing the strange odor in her car, she was horrified by the sight of the unconscious hitchhikers at her side. She screamed in terror, jerked the wheel, and shot off the freeway, bouncing along the shoulder, then dropping into a ditch. At that moment awareness of her condition reached her "gut" level of understanding. There was no other explanation for what had happened, no alternative way to explain the presence of the two males. She was horrified, terrified, and willing to cooperate fully in a cure. She came to the next treatment session totally dedicated to restoring her mental health. Her perseverance eventually helped her to become a whole individual.

Janette's progress was remarkable to me. She went beyond

our therapy and found a way to carry on a verbal dialogue with her personalities. She turned on a tape recorder at home and demanded to speak to her evil alter personality. To my surprise, she recorded a conversation between herself and Lydia, as well as one between herself and a personality I had never met. This was Karen, a personality whose sole job was to help Janette get well.

The incident that prompted the tape recording occurred when Janette was extremely troubled. Someone who identified herself as Janette telephoned my answering service, seemingly in need of help. But when I returned the call, Janette knew nothing about it. She realized that one of the other personalities must have made the call and she was determined to find out which one. She reasoned that since they were all in her head, she could talk to them and they would answer. Her husband set up the tape recorder, then left the house at her request.

"I'm in control, I'm in total control," the tape began. Janette's voice was clear and firm. "I want to talk to Lydia. Lydia, I want to talk to you. I'm in control, I'm in total control. Can you understand that? I want to talk to you, but I'm in control. You have my permission to come out. That's the only time you can come out, when I give permission. I'm in control, I'm in total control, but you have my permission to come out. You have my permission to come out, Lydia."

I listened to this opening of the tape in fascination. I didn't know where Janette got the idea since it wasn't my suggestion and I had never seen such a concept discussed in the literature. However, I was even more surprised when I heard my nemesis, Lydia, say, "Yeah, what do you want?"

An argument between Janette and Lydia followed. Janette accused her alter personality of calling me on the telephone and insisted Lydia tell her why. But Lydia claimed no knowledge of the incident and resented both the accusations and Janette's assumption of power. Finally they both got angry.

"You've lied about everything," Janette told Lydia. "I don't believe you didn't make that phone call and I'm going to find out one way or another why you made the phone call. I'm going to find out what's going on. Now that I'm in control,

I can turn you off and on anytime I want to. You don't have to come out unless I want you to come out. The only time you can come is when I wish you to."

Lydia replied, "You know that's a pack of lies. I can come out any damn time I please. Shit, why should I want to come out anyway around this lousy place. Man, there ain't nothing going on that I want to have anything to do with. Let me tell you one goddamned lousy thing and you'd better listen to it. The next time I do come out, it's gonna be 'cause I want to come out and you're not going to know a thing about it. All of this crap about being in control. You're no more in control now than you ever were, and you know it."

The argument continued, but Lydia was weakened and she knew it. She was coming out with less frequency as Janette began enjoying life more fully. However, Lydia wasn't about to admit defeat. The fact that she wasn't as strong as she had been was hidden in her burst of bravado. She said:

"If I wanted to come out, I'd come out. But I'm just sick and tired of the whole thing. The whole goddamned mess is a drag. I want to tell you something, lady. If I wanted in, I'd come in. But I'm just biding my time. I'm going to come in when I want to, when I have the opportunity that suits me the best, and then, lady, you ain't gonna have nothing to say about it, one way or the other, you ain't gonna have nothing to say about it. Because you know and I know that I'm in control. That crap about you being in control, who'd believe it? Dr. Allison doesn't believe that shit. You're really a pathetic sight. I'm sick and tired of even having anything to do with you. I'm sick of the whole lousy goddamned mess. I'm sick of it. I hate the sight of you. You make me sick. You and your goddamned puritanical ideas. It makes me sick! I don't want to talk to you anymore. I can come and go when I want to."

"Lydia . . . Lydia . . . Lydia . . . Lydia . . . I want to talk to you. I am in control and I want to talk to you, Lydia."

"Dammit, leave me alone. I'm so sick of your whining and bawling and crying and going on that I could just die. You know, as a matter of fact, that's not such a bad idea after all. All these years you've tried to do away with us. All these years and I've stopped you. Yeah, you can thank me for that.

I'm the one that saved us, not you. Shit! You'd have had us in the grave a long time ago, but I'm the one that always pulled us out of it, not you. And when you say that you're the strongest. Dammit! Well, I've got just one good mind to let you do it. I'm sick of it, too. You know I am just as sick as you are of the whole mess. I want out of it, too. But I'll be damned if I'll let you take over. I could have it if I wanted to, mind you, but I just don't want to anymore. I'm just tired, you know."

The subject returned to the telephone call. Lydia tried a new approach. She decided that no telephone call had ever been made to me and tried to convince Janette I was lying to cause her even more trauma. Lydia said:

". . . I didn't make any phone calls, and you didn't make any phone call. You know what's wrong with you? Your mind is going, lady, it's really going. You're so wound up that your mind is slipping right out of it. And you might say that you're my only real help. Because you are helping me to gain everything I wanted, that is, if I want it anymore, which I'm not so sure I do. But it sure is going to be accomplished, because you're the one that did it. You don't know the tricks that are being played on you. That phone call. That Dr. Allison, he's a pretty smart person, he's pretty smart, all right. But he makes a phone call to you—us—and says that you've made a phone call. Well, you know you didn't, and I didn't, but you buy it, and I'm not, and that's the whole difference. You're so damned gullible, you're buying it. That's really hilarious!"

The words seemed to shake Janette's confidence for a moment. However, before she could become too concerned over this new idea, a third voice was heard. It was a new voice to me and I was as surprised by the sound as I had been by the entire experience of hearing a multiple-personality patient have a dialogue with an alter personality.

"Listen to me," said the voice we came to call Karen. "I'm trying to help you. I've been trying to help you, but you won't listen to me."

Janette was shocked. She questioned this new voice, trying to understand what was happening. As they talked, Karen explained that she had called me and that she was trying to help Janette.

"Lydia's not aware. She doesn't know me," Karen said. "But I know Lydia. I know Marie. I know everything that you don't know. I know how to get rid of Lydia. I know why Marie went away. I'm your only hope, if you'll just listen to me. I'm just trying to help you. Because I'm strong. I'm strong but I have to have your confidence and I have to have your belief in me so that we can, you and I, get rid of Lydia for good. I mean from now on, so she can never return again, 'cause she doesn't know me. She's not aware of me. She doesn't know about the phone call."

"What were you going to tell Dr. Allison? Why did you call him? I don't understand. I'm confused . . . I'm so confused. I want to know why."

Karen said, "Because if Dr. Allison knows, if he knows there's two of us against Lydia, then he'll be able to help you better. He'll be able to help you overcome, to overcome Lydia, because she is just one piece of you, and it's a completely bad piece, and we're going to get rid of it."

"But I don't want any more people. I just want me. I just want one personality."

"But don't you understand? If you and I work to help you, we will be one, not two, but just one. But see, I'm the side, I'm the part that can help, if you'll just let me. I'm the part that you fight. You fight me. You use all your energies to fight me when you should be fighting Lydia. You can get rid of her, you know that. You're stronger than she is. But you don't believe you are. You don't believe it. And I know. I know you're stronger."

"I'm scared, I'm so scared," sobbed Janette. "How do I know if I can believe you? I don't know anything more. I'm so confused and mixed up."

"Janette, please trust me. Believe that I am trying to help you, and by helping you, I help myself. Then we can become one and have all the things we want, the good things, the things you know are right. The things that I know are right. We can get rid of her, just knowing that I'm here."

"God help me!" Janette said, weeping uncontrollably.

"Janette, I'm going to be with you and if you can just try to think strong thoughts and hate the kind of person that Lydia is and the things that Lydia has made us do, hate all that she stands for, which is the devil itself. Hate it all and then you and I can become one and be one solid person, solid in every way. Don't be frightened of her. Do whatever I say, to show your feelings, to care, to let yourself go, to let yourself be. Let me please come out. I'm strong, Janette. I'm very, very strong, but you have to want that strength, you have to want it, but let me through, please."

"Okay . . . Okay . . . But will you come out when Dr. Allison talks to me? How can I get you to come out when I want to?"

"Janette, I won't come out like Lydia does. I'm not going to press myself, push myself, because this is something you've got to want to do. You've got to want it yourself. But I will be there to help you. I've got the strength, all the strength that you need, if you'll just allow it. Just let yourself accept it, that you are all the things that Lydia isn't, and that we are two against her one, and that we can become one solid person, that lives, that cares, that knows God."

"I can't think about God anymore! It's too hard to think about it anymore. Why did He let this happen, all this confusion, heartache? I'm scared."

"Janette, you let this happen. You let this happen through all your fears and all the things you did that you thought were bad. You never let yourself see good. But God's there, Janette. He stands by. He's there. You could accept Him. I have."

"Why, why did Marie go away? Why? She was the good one. Why did she go away? She's the one I wanted to be. Why did she go away?"

"Because she's not strong enough, Janette. She's not strong enough. She let people hurt her. They hurt her so bad. She couldn't fight the world. She didn't know how. She knew God. She knew His love and His mercy, but she was too weak. She hurt too bad. She couldn't withstand the pressures and the pain. But you and I can."

"Please come out whenever Dr. Allison needs you to help."

"I am there, Janette, if you will just let me be. I'm there. I've always been there. But I need your strength as much as you need mine. I'm just a part of it, and you're just a part. But together we can be the whole."

When I listened to the tape, I was fascinated. I didn't know who or what Karen might be. I didn't understand how Janette achieved the dialogue she recorded or what its significance might be. I was witness to something that had never been reported in the psychiatric literature as far as I knew. Once again I was on strange terrain in the seemingly endless frontier known as the mind.

I managed to run some psychological tests on Janette; her evil personality, Lydia; the rather bubbly Marie; and the new personality, Karen. The tests were meant to determine the kind of person each entity might be, though they had never been given to a multiple personality before. They were normally used to evaluate emotionally "whole" individuals.

The test results on Marie revealed a person trying desperately to be happy while denying her many problems. Since she had always acted as a long-suffering martyr, this seemed logical.

Lydia proved to be intensely antisocial, while Janette herself was revealed as an extremely depressed, unhappy woman. The only personality who scored in the normal range was Karen. In fact, her test results indicated that she was perfect —absolutely without faults. Since this is not possible with a normal person, the psychologist interpreting the test score evaluation concluded that Karen was trying to hide her faults. In reality, this individual really was "perfect," at least in the areas covered by the tests.

I believe that Karen actually was "perfect" because she was typical of the unique aspect of the mind I eventually found in other multiple-personality patients. She represented the Inner Self Helper—ISH. In a normal person this aspect is the best part of the individual: the conscience or the superego. The definition isn't really important. It is enough to know the ISH is there and that the therapist can call upon it in a multiple personality, utilizing this "individual's" help in the cure.

The Inner Self Helper or ISH might be called the second level of consciousness. The first is the personality we show when dealing with the outside world. Freudian psychiatrists refer to this first level as the ego.

The ISH is that part of the individual's consciousness that is free from emotion. It is not neurotic. It is pure thought and uses good judgment. It has a conscious awareness of God and a strong sense of right and wrong. It does not necessarily respond to cultural demands. As one multiple personality's ISH told me:

"I have many functions. I am the conscience. I am the punisher if need be. I am the teacher, the answerer of questions. I am what she will be, although never completely, for she has her emotional outlets, which I do not need. But she will have my reasoning ability and my ability to look at things objectively. I will always be here and I will always be separate, but the kind of separateness which is yours, a oneness with a very fine line of distinction. An emergency backup, perhaps. If I am gone, she is just a body. She can send part of me off and leave a small portion. But if all is taken, she is a shell. I am kept busy sorting out the different messes and problems created between the alter personalities."

Is this accurate? I don't know. I can only absorb the information given to me and see how it compares from patient to patient. It may be many years before we know how much of this represents reality and how much is simply the notion of a troubled mind. I am only certain that such comments seem to be consistent from patient to patient, adding credibility to what they have to say.

The definitions of the conscious and unconscious mind are probably as varied as the number of psychiatrists. I tend to subscribe to the theories developed by an Italian psychiatrist, Dr. Robert Assagioli, who wrote and taught about a psychotherapeutic approach called psychosynthesis. In his approach, the mind has several levels of consciousness. The first is the conscious mind that contains everything you are aware of at the moment. It might be compared to the tip of an iceberg in that it is probably the smallest part of the mind.

The conscious mind contains a center that is the focus of your attention. However, it retains far more than you are aware of and as a result it is easy to switch from subject to subject. This is very similar to peripheral vision. Even though you may be looking directly at someone, your peripheral vision is catching a glimpse of events occurring on either side of you. The same is true with the mind.

Calling the unconscious a part of the mind is somewhat misleading. We only have one mind and the boundaries between conscious and unconscious are constantly fluctuating. An extremely introspective person is aware of many things that other people might relegate to the unconscious. In other words, it is a matter of what you are thinking and utilizing at the moment as well as what you have buried in your head that, one way or another, can be summoned forth.

The unconscious mind, as I envision it, has three layers—lower, middle, and upper. The lower area is what Freud might call the id. It is the repository of all repressed anger, hostility, and negative emotion. It can be considered the mental "sewer." As it builds, it creates enormous stress for the individual. Lydia might well have originated from this level since she was spewing forth nothing but the hate and venom that Janette repressed.

The middle unconscious is similar to what Freud called the preconscious. It is the storage area for all neutral information. Here you will find telephone numbers you don't need to think about at the moment, the names of all those old friends you haven't seen or thought about for a while, and similarly unemotional information. When you take a test, the facts you suddenly pull out originate from this area. It might even be called the mind's library.

Finally, there is the upper level of the unconscious mind. This is the positive pole, probably where Karen was created. All the mind's coping abilities, musical talents, artistic attributes, and the like are formed there. It is the source of love, appreciation, and truthfulness. All ISH personalities originate here.

During the course of Janette's treatment, we gradually began to piece together her past. Janette was the only child in her family for the first few years of life. Her mother was a cold woman, unable to give affection, and Janette hated her. Janette's father, on the other hand, was extremely physical—touching, loving, and obviously delighting in his infant daughter. She, in turn, thought he was the most wonderful person in the world.

The United States entered World War II when Janette was

just four or five years old. Her father was drafted into the military, a situation he explained to his daughter as best he could. But the child was too young to understand. To her, daddy's several-years-long absence meant only one thing—the man she loved had abandoned her to a woman she despised. She was "unwanted" and the trauma was overwhelming.

Janette's mother had two sisters who were constantly used as object lessons. The sisters were liberated ladies at a time when such a lifestyle was considered sinful by some. At the very least, the sisters liked to drink, dance, and pick up men. But Janette's mother considered them no better than prostitutes.

Her mother believed that a woman's life should be one of martyrdom for husband and family. A woman who took pleasure in life was a fallen individual and she had no intention of letting her daughter engage in such "evil" ways. She was also so ashamed of the "wanton" family members that she warned Janette never to discuss the sisters, or any other shameful secrets, with outsiders. This ingrained lesson later made our therapy difficult because Janette had a hard time talking to me. Only her strong desire to get better encouraged her to remain open, answering my questions so we could better understand the roots of her mental illness.

Janette was elated when her father finally returned from the war. He was thrilled to see how his daughter had grown and they became close companions once more. Unfortunately, her mother became pregnant with the couple's second child. The infant was a boy and her father was delighted with the idea of having a son. To Janette, the baby was a new threat to her security.

The birth of the baby was more pressure than Janette could handle. She knew she was expected to be thrilled about her brother's birth. She had received lectures about loving this new addition to the family. Yet all she could see was her father's joy at having a son—a joy which she felt endangered her relationship with her father. She could not tolerate the notion that she had just regained him after his abandonment for all those years, only to lose his affection to a squealing, crying, prune-faced infant.

Janette was overwhelmed. She wanted to act but couldn't. The pressure built and suddenly Janette receded into her mind. Lydia was born, and Lydia could express all the hate, anger, and frustration Janette couldn't express because of her upbringing. Lydia took the infant boy, cradled him in her arms while her parents smiled indulgently, then horrified them by dropping the child to the floor. They assumed it was a terrible accident and were relieved to find the damage to the baby wasn't serious. In reality, Lydia had hoped to murder the infant by smashing her helpless brother's skull.

When Janette was again in charge of the body, she was shocked to learn that her new brother was injured. Who could have allowed such a terrible thing to happen, she wondered? Surely *she* was not at fault. *She* had not even touched him. But even if she had been holding him, she would be ever so careful because she loved the baby so very much. Mommy said she would love him and mommy was always right.

Sexual relations were another problem area for Janette. Through no fault of her own, her earliest contacts with sex were all negative. The minister of the Fundamentalist church to which her family belonged abused her when she was in elementary school. No one realized how sick he was until he came to Janette's school and lied in order to get her released in his care. Everyone assumed the minister was good and decent. However, he proceeded to try to molest her as soon as they were alone. She fled, her image of God and the church completely shattered. Religion became an object of terror for her after that, since she had assumed that the minister represented the best religion could offer.

The second incident occurred when Janette was approximately eleven years old. She had been playing in the schoolyard after classes, staying by herself until most people had gone home. A boy of fourteen, the class bully, approached her and forced her into the bushes. There he overpowered and raped her.

Janette had been an excellent student until the rape, but after that she lost all interest in class work. She may have equated the sexual abuse with the school, although this was never fully determined. Whatever the case, she wanted to drop out by the time she was in high school. She had been doing less and less school work since the seventh grade, but everyone told her she had to continue until graduation. She didn't want to do that.

Janette responded by creating a stupid alter personality who took her place in classes. The girl was as dumb as Janette was bright. She was genuinely incapable of learning. Her intelligence test scores were low and she lacked the mentality to learn anything. When she reached the age of sixteen, she quit school with her teachers' blessings and took a job as a waitress.

As therapy progressed, I discovered the origin of Marie as well. She had begun as an imaginary playmate for the lonely Janette who was three years old at the time.

Many children have imaginary playmates. It is a normal part of childhood, not a pathological disorder. However, the normal child has a clear understanding of the difference between fantasy and reality. The playmate is not a substitute for real friends when other children are available for play. Furthermore, the imaginary playmate is discarded as the child grows older.

Multiple-personality patients create imaginary playmates without making clear distinctions between fantasy and reality. The playmate becomes quite real to them. Eventually the playmate develops into a genuine personality with certain characteristics, often ones the child dares not show for one reason or another.

For example, Janette was frequently chastised by her mother. She had the feeling that she could do nothing right and was upset by the frequent scoldings she received. She created Marie, who was all-good and never got a scolding. Marie did everything right. She was all-giving, a proper Christian, and the person who would eventually marry and become a mother. Thus, everything positive and good went into Marie and everything negative and hostile went into Lydia.

Sex was a major problem between Janette and her husband, Lee. She was extremely frigid and had trouble touching him in bed. Marie willingly had sex with him, but only because she believed it was her duty, not because she truly enjoyed it.

The only personality with sexual desire was Lydia, and she didn't get along with Lee. She preferred picking up men in bars and delighted in dominating them, making them do whatever she wanted.

My therapy in this area was also based on logic. Janette and Lee professed love for each other and their affection appeared to be genuine. Since sexual relations are a normal expression of love between a husband and wife, I felt it was important to help Janette learn to enjoy sex. I knew enough about her life to realize that her fears were based on her childhood notions of sex and sin. Fortunately, she had been going to P.T.A. meetings for a while and had begun to see that something could be pleasurable without being evil. She agreed to try a desensitization exercise to help her relate to Lee in bed.

Under hypnosis Janette imagined herself on a street with her husband coming toward her. At first he was far away, and she was comfortable with this image. Then I asked her to imagine him at closer range, mentally stopping him where he was if she began to get nervous. She was able to imagine him directly across the street but could not seem to get comfortable with the idea of his being any closer.

During the next desensitization session, I had her imagine herself looking at a video tape of Lee. First he was at the far end of the room. Then she was to use the video camera to bring him closer while she studied his face. Each time she got nervous she could mentally stop the tape. She still saw a color image of Lee but he would not be able to come any closer until she "pushed the button" to let him grow larger. We got to a point where she felt comfortable imagining him as close as six feet away.

Janette's problems with her husband were so severe that we had to go to what seemed almost ridiculous lengths with the imagery. The third session brought Lee to an imaginary position next to her. She was able to imagine touching him while wearing gloves and a heavy coat. Then the imaginary coat came off and she wore only a thin dress. Then the gloves came off and their bare hands touched—one finger at a time. Finally, she imagined them touching four fingers.

Suddenly Janette screamed and began weeping. The mental

imagery had triggered her memory. She was back in elementary school, being raped by the schoolyard bully. At that moment the truth was revealed.

Apparently Janette's mother had not been sympathetic when she learned of the violent abuse her child had experienced. Instead, the mother used the rape incident as an excuse to launch into a tirade against all men. It was terrible to be touched by a man, her mother said. They were all violent animals and it was impossible for the experience to be pleasurable if the woman was at all "decent." The only women who enjoyed the brutal touch of men were prostitutes like Janette's aunts, and they were going straight to the fires of hell!

Janette's new awareness of herself and the source of her strong emotions helped change her attitude toward both sex and Lee. She was able to have normal relations with him and actually came to enjoy sex with the man she loved.

And so we worked, step by step, toward sound mental health. We identified traumas through the use of hypnosis and other techniques. Often one memory led to another and we delved deeper and deeper into her past. As we learned what had happened and how she had originally coped, we explored new ways of coping. She learned to express a full range of emotions and reject the warped value system of her emotionally disturbed mother.

Some of the memories were shocking. I realized that a mental illness as extreme as multiple personality had to stem from overwhelming traumas, but the idea that one person could endure so much suffering was something even a psychiatrist does not want to think about.

For example, Janette had a pair of earrings that greatly troubled her. She avoided wearing them because she was so uncomfortable when she put them on. Yet Janette could not remember where she had gotten them and assumed they were from a dime store or a gift from Lee. However, when Janette was finally able to focus on the source, she remembered that they were a present—from the men who had gang-raped her.

Janette had been in a mental hospital where the attendants were as sick as the patients. Several of them became interested in Janette, although in fairness I have to assume that Lydia may have led them on. The men forced Janette to have intercourse with each of them against her will. When they were finished they gave her a pair of earrings, to bribe her into silence. We were never able to determine whether Janette feared another attack or thought no one would believe an inmate over an attendant. However, she said nothing, took the earrings with her when she left the hospital, then suppressed the incident. The earrings served as a constant, subtle reminder, preying on her subconscious, until we worked through the incident and threw away the earrings.

Another time Janette awakened to find her own mother beginning to molest her sexually. The mother, who was obviously a very disturbed woman, apparently had incestuous tendencies toward her daughter. Fortunately, after Janette awakened, the mother did not press her desires and returned to her own room.

Memory after memory was brought to the conscious mind and explored. Janette learned new ways to view the situation and alternative methods of coping.

Janette was still in therapy when she came to tell me that she and Lee were leaving town. They were moving to another state where he had a chance at a job he wanted to take.

The idea of the move frightened me. Janette was well on her way to recovery, but she wasn't healthy yet. I knew it would be difficult for her to find another psychiatrist, especially considering the rarity of the illness.

Janette has since made a full recovery. She corresponded with me for several months, participating in "therapy" by mail since she refused even to look for another doctor. As she grew stronger, she also faced tragedy. Lee left her after she discovered he was carrying on with other women. Then she fell in love with a man whom she wanted to marry, but an automobile accident left him confined to a wheelchair. He also left her, for what he considered a noble reason. He did not wish married life to be a burden for the woman he loved. He thought it was better that she find a "whole" man. She disagreed with his reasoning yet couldn't convince him to change his mind.

Now Janette and her children are on their own and I hear

from her periodically. She tells me that she is functioning successfully on her own. She did not create an alter personality to handle her love life and she has not created anyone for her current existence. She is coping as everyone else does, facing the ups and downs of life as a whole individual.

And so my career with multiple-personality patients began. Janette had forced me to take the first few steps into a mental universe which few psychiatrists ever enter. I knew my future would be quite different from anything I had previously imagined. I had taken a giant step into the unknown and my exploration was just beginning.

Chapter 3

Carrie, Who Chose to Die

I was sleeping soundly when the first rings penetrated my brain. It was around two in the morning on a winter's day early in 1973 and my first reaction was to bury my head in the pillow until the noise stopped. But after the third ring I realized that this was an hour when depressed people often reach an extremely low point. Restaurants are closed. Bars are closed. Movie theaters and bowling alleys are generally locked for the night. There is no place to go for companionship, and the blackness of the night seems to increase the feeling of isolation from others. It is a time when people contemplate suicide and some actually pick up a razor blade, a gun, or poison. If one of my patients had reached this point, he or she might be telephoning me as a cry for help.

I quickly rolled from my bed, grabbed the telephone receiver, and identified myself. Adrenaline began surging through my body, making me tense and alert. If this was one of my patients, I would have to be alert. I couldn't allow myself to fail. The potential consequences were too grim.

"This is the coroner's office, Dr. Allison," said the voice on the other end of the line. "I'm sorry to bother you at this hour, but . . ."

I barely heard the words that followed. My stomach muscles tensed and I felt nauseated. I began to sweat and my hands became cold. I had all the symptoms of shock, although I was too numb to realize it.

The person on the other end of the line was very business-like. One of my patients, Carrie Hornsby, had been found dead in her home from an overdose of drugs and alcohol. The coroner's office got my name from her husband and thought I would want to know.

Psychiatrists aren't supposed to cry. We are supposed to present masks of indifference, listening to stories of extreme child abuse, sexual deviation, and incredible torments without showing a reaction. We are never to judge anyone. We must not inflict our value systems on our patients. We aren't to get involved in a patient's personal life. In effect, we must deny our own humanity and compassion during the hour we share with the troubled individuals who daily enter our offices.

I suppose some of my colleagues might criticize my reactions that night. They would probably prefer the attitude of the coroner's office—that death is an aspect of life that must be faced calmly.

However, it was easier for the coroner's office to handle the situation with such cool professionalism. They had been called to deal with a body—a lump of skin, bone, hair, and blood. The form they saw was human but it had no more life or personality than a department store mannequin. For them Carrie was a cipher, a statistic to be numbered and placed in the record books for that year. They never knew Carrie as a living, breathing individual. They had never heard her infectious laugh on those days when her spirits were high and the world seemed to her to be the most marvelous place in the universe in which to exist. They never watched the way her long, flaming red hair bounced against her shoulders as she walked. They had never listened to her hopes and dreams, nor had they ever shared her anguish and the internal "demons" of her mind that made her want to scream endlessly. But I had.

I was sick and filled with self-loathing when I hung up the telephone. Perhaps I had deluded myself into believing that our therapy sessions were helping her maintain emotional stability and cope with life in a constructive manner. I had not detected the signs that she was suicidal. In fact, I had congratulated myself that her therapy was going so well. And now she was dead. . . .

Salt tears burned my eyes as I grieved for Carrie. Yet at

the same time I was thinking about her case and the events I had been involved in just prior to her death. Part of me mourned and part of me tried to deny the reality of my apparent failure.

Sleep was impossible that night. All my thoughts were of Carrie, one of the most beautiful women I had ever seen, who was also cursed with the same mental illness I had first encountered with Janette. Carrie was the second of my multiple-personality cases.

Carrie Hornsby came to my office with a history of frequent, severe depressions and mood disorders. For many years she had acted in a manner that her family thought was odd, but they had never paid much attention to her behavior until New Year's Eve, 1972. On that night she failed to show up at a party and her husband, Randolph, discovered her in the apartment of another man.

Randolph Hornsby was a violent, self-centered individual who believed that it was Carrie's duty to accept anything he might wish to do. The idea that she might want to have an affair shocked him and he grew livid. When he was through having his way, she went into the bathroom, took a razor blade, and tried to slash her wrists.

Nothing seemed especially unusual about Carrie's case when she first walked through the door, although physically she was one of the most beautiful women I had ever met. She was extremely tall and slender, and her magnificent, flaming red hair enhanced her lovely face. She was the kind of woman who appeared to be completely carefree. I certainly never would have thought that I'd have to develop special techniques, including exorcism, to help Carrie.

I had another reaction to Carrie that was neither objective nor reasoned, although I now realize it was somewhat prophetic. I had the odd feeling that this young woman was going to play a unique role in my life. She would influence my work, my emotions, or some other aspect of my existence, although I didn't know how or why and certainly couldn't rationally analyze the feeling. Had I known just how prophetic that reaction was to prove, I don't think I would have fully believed it. Future events would prove too painful and bizarre to have been anticipated on the basis of my previous experiences as a psychiatrist.

Carrie had always been beautiful. Even as a child, her long hair and radiant face delighted everyone who saw her. All the relatives doted on her, paying constant attention to her. Despite this attention, her early childhood was unusually pressured.

Her father was a career Navy officer who traveled constantly. Her mother developed a brain tumor when Carrie was a newborn infant, a condition requiring radiation therapy with all its accompanying nausea and other side effects. As a result, Carrie was passed around to her aunts, uncles, and other relatives. She spent the most time with her grandparents, one of whom, her father's mother, had severe emotional problems herself.

As I developed more of an understanding of multiple-personality patients, I discovered that all either have been unwanted by one or both parents or have perceived that such a situation existed. In Carrie's case, her mother genuinely did not want her. Her conception was an accident, and her mother had hoped that Carrie would spontaneously abort.

Carrie's father was a military man who was seldom at home. He was eventually transferred to Japan but could not handle Carrie without the help of his wife who was too sick to be of assistance. Both parents agreed to let Carrie's grandmother and grandfather raise her during this period.

When Carrie was six months old, the radiation treatment proved successful and the entire family was reunited in Japan. Unfortunately, this placed a number of emotional pressures on Carrie. She felt abandoned by her grandparents, the primary source of love and affection she had known since birth. Her father was away from the house on a regular basis, her mother was still weak, and Carrie was being raised by Japanese help who neither spoke the same language nor had much interest in her. There was tremendous hostility among the Japanese people toward Americans at this time, so the family lived in an isolated, guarded area with other Americans. There were few small children so Carrie spent much of her time without real friends.

While in Japan, Carrie developed the habit of pulling chunks of her beautiful red hair from her head, putting them in her mouth, and swallowing. Her mother took her to the base physician, who provided a simple answer. Carrie couldn't pull her hair if she had none, therefore her head should be completely shaved.

Having one's head shaved at nineteen months, Carrie's age at the time, would be a shock to anyone. But Carrie had other emotional traumas to bear. She was unwanted and, for all practical purposes, had been emotionally abandoned. When her mother finally did spend some time with her, it was only long enough to handle the shaving of her hair, an action Carrie perceived as unspeakably brutal. Carrie was horrified by what was happening to her. She was angry, frightened, and desperately wanted to flee. She twisted and turned her tiny body, trying to escape her mother's grasp as the scissors and a razor reduced her to a "skin-head." She screamed in terror, overwhelmed by circumstances she could neither understand nor escape.

Her mind took the action that her body could not. Carrie retreated into the recesses of her brain and Wanda was created.

Wanda was born into violence, filled with hatred and capable of acting out all the anger Carrie was unable to express. Wanda was destined to treat the world as disdainfully as she perceived herself to be treated. She would hurt people any way she could.

From that point on, Carrie's mental problems became increasingly severe. Throughout her childhood and adolescence, she faced a number of traumatic episodes and she continued to cope by creating alter personalities.

When she was four years old, she and her sister spent most of their time playing with the children of a serviceman on temporary overseas duty. These children, a girl and a boy just one year older than Carrie, were rather rough. One afternoon Carrie's sister and the girl wandered off by themselves, leaving four-year-old Carrie with the boy. He promptly began beating her, then wrestled her to the ground and sat on her chest.

Carrie was terrified, unable to breathe with the little boy

sitting on her. She beat him with her fists, kicked and struggled ineffectually, all the time becoming weaker and weaker from lack of air. She was only semiconscious by the time he got off. In her panic, she mentally created a male aspect. This was not an alter personality, although it eventually became one. In a sense, she was setting the groundwork for what would become a full split.

This male aspect of Carrie's mind was the result of what is known as identification with the aggressor. It is a normal defense mechanism in extreme circumstances. When a person is hurt by someone and feels helpless, he or she may psychologically alter the circumstances in order to feel safe. A girl who has been beaten by a boy who is a bully may imagine herself a boy too, since boys cause pain and girls are their victims. If she can be the boy, she won't have to suffer again.

The identification with the aggressor is usually a temporary problem. However, in Carrie's case, the male aspect was strengthened by an experience that occurred while she was living on her grandmother's ranch.

Her grandmother, her father's mother, was a man-hater who wanted nothing to do with any male other than her own son. She hired only girls to work on the ranch, and at least some of them were lesbians. In Carrie's associations with these women, she often played the butch or male role, and in this way she strengthened the male aspect she had developed in her childhood.

Carrie felt like an outsider at the ranch. She didn't particularly care for her grandmother or the other girls. In fact, she wanted as little to do with people in general as possible. Her one real pleasure was a horse her grandmother had given her. Carrie rode that horse every chance she got. She'd often sneak to the stables at night, take the horse without being seen, and ride him for hours. Unfortunately, this habit was to result in the formation of another alter personality.

It happened late one night when Carrie had difficulty sleeping. There was a full moon and she thought it would be fun to ride out to the nearby lake where she could look up at the stars. She didn't realize that a group of outlaw motorcycle riders were in the area. As soon as she reached the lake they were upon her, forcing her to drink some of the liquor they carried with them. After a few minutes of this "party," they pushed her to the ground and took turns holding and raping her. It was her first sexual experience and it was a horrible one. Again her mind was overwhelmed when her body couldn't flee the assault. Again she created another personality.

Carrie never reported the rape and even managed to suppress the memory of it. She was terrified that if her grandmother knew what she had done—sneaking out with her horse—the animal would be taken from her. That horse meant more to her than anything else in the world and she couldn't risk his loss. She kept silent, forcing herself to forget the rape.

Seth was Carrie's first serious boyfriend in high school. They went together for over a year before he suggested they have sex together. She refused, becoming panicky when he made the proposal. She had managed to suppress completely any memory of the rape but his request created a sense of fear in her mind. She didn't know why the idea of intercourse terrified her, since she loved Seth, but she couldn't do it. He was frustrated and told her that he wouldn't continue the relationship without sex. When she still said no, he stopped seeing her.

Soon Carrie began dating Randolph Hornsby, one of the most disreputable boys in her high school. The entire family was notorious in the area. There was talk of various crimes they had committed. The men in the family would fight over anything, and they were frequently drunk and belligerent.

Carrie's family was upset by her relationship with Randolph, but there was little they could do about it. Carrie had felt unwanted and alienated from her family for several years. As a result, she clung to Randolph, determined to keep him.

After only a few dates, Randolph told Carrie that he was going to have sex with her. She was terrified, although again she didn't know why. She also realized that if she didn't do it, she would lose him just as she had lost the previous boyfriend. As he started to unbutton her blouse, she seemed to lose consciousness.

The next thing Carrie knew, Randolph was bringing her home. From his comments she gathered that she had been extremely active during their sexual relations, even though she had thought she was still a virgin. She had to assume they had had sex, but she could not remember doing it. What she did not know, and I did not find out until well into therapy, was that sex was enjoyed by a new personality who had been created specifically for that purpose. That personality would become a man-chaser with an insatiable sexual appetite, although always without Carrie's knowledge.

All this information about Carrie did not come out during our first meeting, nor did I learn the truth about her condition during the next several sessions. Carrie was deeply troubled, but otherwise seemed quite normal. I assumed the solution to her problems would be fairly simple. Janette was my multiple-personality "quota" for my lifetime. I had chanced to meet one, an experience most psychiatrists would never encounter, and I certainly couldn't imagine facing another such case. Thus, I never once suspected there might be anything more seriously wrong with Carrie.

I still remember the day I discovered Carrie's real problem. She was very upset when she entered my office. She told me that she liked to walk along the beach by the ocean. Lately when she did this, she would suddenly find herself walking in the water. Often the water was up to her chest or even her chin before she became aware of what was happening. She had to swim back, terrified that she would drown, apparently by her own hand, yet with no knowledge of leaving the beach and wading into the water.

Carrie's actions seemed as strange to me as they did to her. I had known of patients who tried to commit suicide by walking into the water but they always knew what they were doing. It was a deliberate act with full awareness.

Carrie's unexplained problems were particularly upsetting because of the responsible position she held at the time of the difficulty. She worked as a nurse at an alcoholic treatment center and needed to be alert to patient problems constantly.

The job created even more stress because the doctor who ran the place was highly disreputable. He managed to convince Carrie to have oral sex with him in his office. Although the door was always closed, his wife, who worked for the center, was usually typing just outside. After Carrie satisfied the doctor's lust, he would bill her for the office visit as though she was a patient in addition to being an employee. She actually paid the bills.

In an effort to help Carrie discover why she was walking into the water, I suggested we try hypnosis. I hoped that would force her to concentrate on the incident and reveal the truth. I assumed that she had been aware of her action at the time and had willed herself to forget because she was too embarrassed or ashamed about it. I certainly didn't expect to discover what happened next.

"She's going to kill me," Carrie said. Her voice was filled with fear as she talked about this unseen but very real person living inside her head. She had some knowledge of this other party within her, although this was long before she could understand that the evil "person" was just another aspect of herself.

I started to say something but Carrie kept talking. "She's going to kill me. She took a bunch of pills at work and she's going to kill me."

The mention of pills concerned me as much as the shock of what was being said. I knew how easy it would have been for Carrie to steal pills from the alcoholic treatment center. As a nurse, she had access to patient medication prescribed by the doctor. It would have been easy for her to pocket the medicine meant for a patient, then write a note on the patient's chart indicating that the medicine had been properly distributed.

"She's going to kill me this weekend. She's got all those pills from work stashed away in my house. She plans to overdose this weekend and kill me."

"Who's going to kill you?" I asked.

"Wanda. Wanda's going to kill me."

I was confused. I had never once thought about the possibility of multiple personality until this point. Janette was currently undergoing treatment and I "knew" she was to be my one and only encounter.

"Who is Wanda?" I asked. Perhaps she was paranoid. Perhaps there was another nurse named Wanda whom Carrie perceived as having a grudge against her.

Suddenly Carrie's posture changed. Her beautiful face seemed to harden and distort. Her body tensed, as though braced for a fight. She seemed mad at the world and was totally unlike the Carrie I knew.

"*I'm* Wanda, you fat-headed son of a bitch!"

And then I knew. I couldn't comprehend how or why, but somehow I had two multiple-personality patients, not only during the course of my career, but at the same time. It had to be a first for the medical journals, but at that moment I wasn't too enthusiastic about the idea of setting records. What I really wanted to do was run, get into some other field. Maybe I could work on an assembly line somewhere, doing a routine job for eight hours. If I could have sent Carrie to another doctor, I would have referred her the moment I got the main personality back.

I talked with Wanda for a while, unsure of what to say or do. We discussed the suicide plans and I had the distinct impression that Wanda wanted to live. She just didn't like sharing the body with the others and felt that if she could kill them, she would have the body all to herself. She had no compunction about murder. It was a means to an end that she felt justified in taking.

After several minutes of conversation, I convinced Wanda that she would suffer too. She didn't like what I said, nor did she want to believe it. Since Carrie eventually did take her life, it is obvious that she had retained the option of suicide/murder in her mind. However, before she left the office that day, I was convinced that she was no longer in immediate danger.

I had a long talk with Carrie that afternoon. I told her that I knew why she was having such bizarre experiences. I did not present my diagnosis of multiple personality, however, because I planned to explain that phenomenon during the following week's visit. I decided to invite Janette to that session in the hope that she could help Carrie adjust to the idea.

Carrie was only of average intelligence and, though a nurse, had little psychology training. It was difficult for her to comprehend what I was trying to say, although what she did grasp terrified her. She handled the stress in what had become her routine way—she created a new personality for coping with the rest of that session.

Janette offered a contrast to my explanation although it did nothing to alleviate Carrie's mounting fear. Janette also lacked psychology training, but she could relate some of her own experiences to Carrie. The blackout spells and other aspects of Janette's unusual existence were typical of Carrie's own experiences. The end result was that Janette became a friend and counselor to Carrie, able to understand the other woman even though she was too troubled to do more than lend a sympathetic ear.

Carrie's face didn't show any change as I explained the multiple-personality concept to her. She nodded from time to time, always watching me intensely. Everything seemed fine on the surface. What I couldn't see was a mounting internal hysteria that was overwhelming her. She was unable to cope with my words and reacted by forming an alter personality.

I accepted the reality of all this at the time of treatment. However, as I began to see other patients with similar problems, I came to realize that alter personalities do not instantly appear in public. They have a period of gestation, so to speak, during which they develop full force. Only then do they have a unique thought pattern, body attitude, and all the other characteristics that make someone an individual. Before this occurs, they do have an awareness of the outside world and a general consciousness of what is going on around them. However, they cannot actually be identified as a personality.

This new personality did not need the usual gestation period. Someone new had to control the body and this personality took over immediately. She had not developed into a full character with unique likes and dislikes, but she was able to serve the purpose for which she had been created—getting Carrie through my office session and away from the building.

During a later therapy session I met Carrie's new personality. She entered my office, shoulders hunched, her head in her hands. She spread her fingers, peeking through them and smiling impishly. "Hello," she said in a tiny little girl's voice much higher than Carrie's. "Who are you?" She giggled, then put her hand to her mouth.

"Carrie?" I asked, realizing full well that this was someone new.

"Carrie's not here," said the new personality, giggling again. "Who are you? Are you my daddy?"

Indeed I was. This new personality, whom I named Debra, had been developed in my office. She believed Janette and I were her parents since we were the first adults she had ever met. She was extremely childlike, yet seemed to protect Carrie from any new hurts, including, for the moment, facing the truth about her illness.

Debra eventually began to visit Janette from time to time, always acting as though Janette was her mother. Fortunately, Janette accepted Carrie/Debra since even so bizarre a circumstance was easier to handle than the reality of her own illness.

I had no idea how one patient, still in therapy, might interact with another patient who shared the same extreme illness. However, once I introduced them, it was out of my hands, since Debra took it upon herself to go to Janette's home. The situation didn't seem to hurt Carrie in any way and it may have strengthened Janette's determination to get better. She could understand her own behavior through her observations of the changes in Carrie's condition. Faced with another person's bizarre behavior pattern, her own actions, related by others, became both more real and less tolerable. Janette never again wanted to be plagued by an illness that could create such unusual living circumstances.

I, personally, was horrified that I had misjudged Carrie's mental state so badly. I wanted to think that I was a better doctor than to have compounded her problems with another personality. But like it or not, I was her "daddy" and Janette became "mommy." Quite by accident, I had been handed an instant "daughter."

Debra, my new "daughter," behaved totally like a child. She giggled continually and had none of the sexual feelings normally associated with an adult woman. She also seemed to age as I knew her. Eventually she told me that she felt the first stirrings of sexual desire and wanted my advice about what it meant and how to handle it.

Despite her childishness, Debra took on an increasingly

important role as Carrie's rescuer. Whenever Carrie or one of the other personalities attempted to commit suicide, Debra would take control and get help. Sometimes she would take charge just before Carrie could take a lethal overdose of pills of one sort or another. Other times she would take control when Carrie tried to slash her wrists, driving the "body" to the hospital Emergency Room for help.

During the next few sessions, Carrie seemed more inclined to face her mental problems. She admitted that people called her by different names at times, and she seemed to have different behavior patterns for each name. I asked her if she could define the matter any better and she said she would try.

At a later session, Carrie brought a long list into my office. It was made up of about fifteen different subjects, including, among others, preferences in food, dress, and entertainment. Four names—Carrie, Wanda, Sandra, and Naomi appeared on the list, and each name was connected to a list of subjects, indicating the personalities' differing tastes in all kinds of activities. I remember that one of the personalities liked me, another feared me, a third hated me, and the fourth wanted to help me solve Carrie's problems.

The list made me aware of one of the most unusual aspects of multiple-personality cases. The mind is an odd resource of information. Carrie genuinely had amnesia during the periods when her alter personalities took charge. She did not know what they did or whom they were with, and they also seemed to share this amnesia about each other for the most part. However, in most cases, one aspect of the mind, the Inner Self Helper, coordinates everything. Apparently Carrie had gone home and this aspect of her mind had taken control in order to prepare the list identifying the four personalities.

Carrie found the list of personalities and their traits and brought it to me. She was so accustomed to unexplained events that the discovery of the list seemed a rather minor surprise. She didn't know how it got there, although intellectually she assumed it was the result of her illness. She only knew that I was supposed to have it, so she brought it to me.

Carrie never seemed to get past the intellectual acceptance of her illness. She failed to have the kind of "gut" experience that Janette had reached with the hitchhikers. Carrie worked at getting better and was becoming increasingly able to cope with life, but ultimately that did not prove to be adequate. Had she been able to accept her illness completely, with the accompanying desire to get well, perhaps she might have lived. I will never know.

Because Carrie never had a "gut" acceptance of her illness, and because she had several serious personal hang-ups which made her condition even more severe, I was forced to develop a series of highly unorthodox treatments during the course of her therapy.

One of her biggest hang-ups was her belief that she would choke to death. Before I had even met her, she had been hospitalized because she had refused to eat. At the time she had a strong will to live, and she was so sure that she would choke on some food that she decided the only way to survive was to starve herself. The severity of her delusion was such that even though she was in nursing school at the time, she didn't realize that the consequence of starvation was death.

The psychiatrist who was then treating Carrie was able to get her to eat again, but could not alleviate her fears. She was also convinced that she would die on New Year's Eve in 1973, a belief that was somehow related to the fear of choking. There seemed to be no special significance attached to the date, yet she was sure it would happen.

Toward the end of 1972, Carrie and I began to explore an area most psychiatrists never even think about. Even now I wonder how and why I did what I did. I still hesitate to discuss this aspect of the case with my colleagues, although I have since learned, during discussions at meetings of the several psychiatric and hypnosis associations to which I belong, that others faced similar problems.

At the time, Carrie was in and out of the hospital as a result of depression and drug and alcohol abuse. She had a close friend, another nurse, who was frequently with her, and this nurse told me an amazing story.

The nurse involved was an avid student of parapsychology. She claimed to have psychic ability and had involved herself with parapsychological experiments. These involved attempts to read someone else's thoughts under controlled conditions via ESP; attempts to determine the sequence in which different playing cards would be uncovered from a deck; and similar tests of a type conducted by researchers throughout the country.

The nurse came to me one day and confided an unusual experience she had had in one of the mind dynamics courses she had taken. The course had lasted two weekends, and the incident had occurred on the last day.

The course instructor had been discussing the concept of mentally "entering" the mind of another individual in order to learn what was troubling that person. Each person at the session went into a trance, concentrating on visualizing the person he or she wanted to understand better. They could then relate what they "saw" within that individual.

The instructor demonstrated his own ability to do this and asked his students to provide names of troubled individuals whom they knew. Then he put himself into a trance and described what he "found" in that person's head.

The nurse told me that she gave the instructor Carrie's full name and physical description, but claimed she told him nothing else about Carrie. She did not mention that Carrie was my patient or that multiple personality was an aspect of her problem.

The instructor had been talking calmly about each person he "visited." However, when he concentrated on Carrie, he became highly agitated. He broke out of the trance and said he couldn't get into her mind. He said that the nurse should not try either because it was too dangerous.

The nurse was curious. Had this man been a fortune teller or a phony, she would have ignored the matter. But he had been straight with everyone and this was the first time he had acted so strangely. She went to him after the session and asked what he had "seen."

According to her, the instructor had witnessed some sort of evil force. He saw red and black rather than an actual being, but he had the sense that he was viewing a depraved drug addict who had died and was using Carrie's body. He also mentioned the name Bonnie Pierce or Price—he wasn't sure which—who had died of a drug overdose in New York City in 1968. The late Ms. Pierce or Price was in her twenties at the time and it was her soul, essence, or spirit which had entered Carrie. Since Carrie was also a drug abuser, her body would have been eminently suitable for a takeover.

I greeted this information about spirit possession with more skepticism than many of my colleagues might have, although I knew of no one at the time who was both a serious psychiatrist and a believer in possession. The reason for my skepticism was my background. My father disdained the emotional aspects of religion, including the concept of possession, and he would have little to do with it.

My father's influence, along with my own life experiences, had shaped my own beliefs. When the nurse approached me with her story about Carrie, I was obviously skeptical. My first step was to treat the matter with scientific curiosity. Carrie was troubled, there was no doubt about that. The cause of her problem was unknown, but one individual, supposedly "in tune" with her mind, had come up with the "cause." He supplied a first name and two last names, as well as the city in which the "possessing spirit" had once lived. I decided to gather all the possible facts before coming to any conclusion.

I wrote to the various records departments in New York City to see if I could get a death record on Bonnie Pierce or Price. I gave the 1968 death date but asked them to search the records for many months before and after the supposed time of death. The results were negative. There were no records anywhere. If the story were true, something was not quite accurate, whether the date, name, or location. More likely it was the rambling of a charlatan professor. So much for spirit possession! Score one point for the scientists! Or so I thought. . . .

While all this was going on, Carrie was becoming increasingly desperate. Things were happening to her that were both outside her memory and seemingly beyond her control. She was physically abusing her body with drugs and discovering herself in circumstances that were often dangerous or embarrassing. Her nerves were on edge. She begged and pleaded for help but everything I tried to do for her seemed useless. Her life was becoming a nightmare, completely out of control. I had accepted responsibility for helping her, yet had exhausted all the usual techniques. I needed to do something different, if only to give her hope. And that's when my thoughts again turned to Bonnie. I wondered what would happen if I took the idea of spirit possession more seriously.

Despite my skepticism at the time, I believed then, and still believe, that a good psychiatrist must be open to new ideas. The welfare and eventual cure of the patient must be his only consideration, and when conventional techniques fail, he must be willing to explore new options. Often, an unorthodox treatment can be very useful if a patient is suffering from a persistent delusion. For example, if a patient believes little green men are attacking him, a psychiatrist will not be able to persuade him otherwise through the use of reason or logic. After all, the patient *is* seeing the little green men. Only if the psychiatrist accepts and works with that belief can the patient begin to improve. And it is an essential component in gaining the patient's trust. For a psychiatrist, there is only one "reality"—that of the patient.

Skillful therapists in alcohol treatment centers use this principle instinctively. When the patient is undergoing detoxification, he or she will frequently "see" snakes or other creatures emerging from the walls. The therapist won't try to argue; instead, he or she will take some weapon, perhaps a shoe, and strike the wall, "killing" the snakes. The alcoholic feels better and accepts the therapist as a friend. It is unorthodox, but it is a technique necessary to help that patient at that moment.

With these thoughts in mind, I decided to give the concept of spirit possession a try. Carrie was desperate and she wasn't responding to any of the textbook techniques I had tried. I told her I had a new idea that might help her and she agreed readily.

Spirit possession is not part of a psychiatrist's school curriculum. When I decided to accept Bonnie as a spirit and perform an exorcism, I knew I was breaking with tradition. And I realized that the contemporary psychiatric literature would be useless.

An early session with Carrie had revealed, among other

things, that she had once experimented with witchcraft while in high school. She had also once had a boyfriend who was serious about "black magic." Her involvement appeared to be typical of the seemingly silly things many high school students do and it did not worry me. However, it did indicate that she believed in the concept of good and evil, of God and the devil. Thus, I felt that a religious approach such as an exorcism would appeal to her, although I had no intention of talking about Bonnie beforehand. I didn't want to place the idea in her mind, creating a problem where none existed, if that proved to be the case.

I went to the Bible and began reading about possession. The New Testament discusses Christ's casting out of demons and I chose to follow this concept. It seemed fairly simple as I interpreted it. An exorcist must call out each demon by name, then command it to leave in the name of the Holy Trinity—Christ, God the father, and the Holy Spirit.

It is important to remember that religion and mental health are not as contradictory as they may seem. In earlier times, the church cared for the mentally ill. The fact that doctors have taken over this function doesn't mean that bringing religion to a treatment program is wrong. Essentially, I was bringing mental health full circle, combining the best of medicine and religion. Since my family has produced a long line of ministers, it seemed quite natural for me to mix a religious act with my psychiatry since this seemed to be in the best interest of my patient.

My first step was to hypnotize Carrie in the presence of another doctor, a friend who was interested in watching me try this unorthodox approach. He held a tape recorder to insure a complete record of anything that might happen, as well as lending his presence to provide moral support.

Once Carrie was hypnotized, I talked to her about her life experiences and asked if a Bonnie was present. I tried to imply that Bonnie might be just another personality. Carrie was aware of her ailment, so my mention of the name was not likely to trigger the creation of such a personality. I did not want to hint at the idea of an outside spirit. She told me that no Bonnie was there.

After giving Carrie plenty of time to expose Bonnie, if indeed Bonnie existed at all outside that instructor's imagination, I was ready to give up. Nothing had happened and the entire episode made me feel a little foolish. It seemed a bad idea to have gone this far, although I knew my patient would not be hurt by my actions.

The doctor who was assisting me took a piece of paper and wrote a note suggesting that I go deeper than hypnosis. I had no idea what he meant but I later learned that his suggestion resulted from a course he had taken. He was told that if hypnosis doesn't produce the desired results, the subject can be taken to a deeper level where almost anything might happen.

I literally suggested to Carrie that she enter a deeper level, which she apparently did. I don't know how she did it. I don't really know what happened. This type of situation has not come up again, and at the time I was interested in results, not reasons.

Next, I asked Carrie if someone named Bonnie was influencing her life. This time she said yes. She also became highly agitated. She told me she wanted to get rid of Bonnie and her words were an agonized plea.

My voice grew deep and authoritative. I felt that an exorcist would have to be a strong, commanding person in full charge of every situation. His booming rhetoric would act as a conduit for God's healing power, terrorizing the spirit and forcing it to leave. If that was Carrie's idea of an exorcist as well, then my approach would be perfect.

"Above your head is a crystal ball," I stated in a booming voice. I was holding a crystal ball on a chain, a souvenir I had received from one of the hypnosis courses I had taken. It had no significance except a symbolic one. "I command Bonnie to leave Carrie's body and enter this crystal ball. In the name of God, the Son, and the Holy Ghost, Bonnie—leave Carrie, leave Carrie in peace! I command you, Bonnie, leave Carrie! By all that's holy, leave Carrie! Leave Carrie in peace and depart for wherever you go! Wherever spirits go, go there and leave Carrie! When the crystal ball stops swinging, then Bonnie will be gone and Carrie will be at peace."

I thought the last was a nice touch. Of course, I was holding the string as still as I could so the ball couldn't move. Or could it?

I glanced at the crystal and noticed that it was moving in a circle with a centrifugal force all its own. I was surprised. I looked at my hand and it appeared to be steady, yet that ball was rotating fairly rapidly.

"All right, Carrie, as soon as Bonnie is gone from you, tell me 'yes' by raising your right index finger." The raising of the finger had nothing to do with the exorcism, but is a standard device in hypnosis. By designating one finger as a "yes" finger and another as a "no" finger, the patient can answer questions easily since speech is often an effort during hypnosis.

Suddenly the crystal ball began slowing. As it did, Carrie raised her "yes" finger, signaling me that Bonnie was gone. Then I said, "All right, Carrie, your work is done. I want you to rest as long as you need to. When you open your eyes and awaken, you will be a new person. You will be the person you want to be, with the strength, the wisdom, and the knowledge that will be best for you. You will be free from the crippling handicap you've carried and you will have the ability to handle whatever new problems come into your path, just as you've overcome this problem, the biggest hurdle of your life, and you've done it well. Now we will let you rest and you can come back when you feel right and ready for it. When you have gone through whatever resolution you must go through in your mind, you'll be the best person that you have the capacity to be."

The entire exorcism took approximately two and one half minutes. Ten minutes later I talked with Carrie, who commented, "I've always thought there was something, a spirit or a vision or a shadow of something, always with me. But it's not there now. I used to hate to close my eyes because I'd see it. Just a haunting evil feeling that I'm going to die. It was separate from the feeling of wanting to die because of the hell of all this [she meant the multiple personalities]. This is a different feeling than I've had for a long time. Now I feel like there is hope where I didn't feel like that before."

I was pleased by Carrie's remarks but rather uneasy about myself and the entire experience. I know what I saw and it was corroborated by the other doctor. Yet there were so many questions. Was Carrie possessed? Did the crystal ball spin because of "Bonnie" or did it spin because I twirled the string unconsciously? Carrie later said that while I held the ball over her head, she felt some force move up through her body and out through her head. Yet the other doctor and I were watching Carrie intently. If my hand had spun the string ever so slightly, I would not have noticed, although it probably would have been enough to cause the ball to swing as it did.

What is the answer? I don't know. All I can say is that Carrie lost her fear of impending death by choking. She no longer worried about New Year's Eve and nothing happened to her during that time. As far as I was concerned, if my actions helped my patient progress toward a normal, integrated personality, they were a success. However, I had no intention of embarrassing myself in front of my colleagues by admitting the experiment.

During the treatment, Wanda began appearing with increasing frequency. She hated Carrie and despised Carrie's husband. (Wanda never married anyone. That was Carrie's "mistake.") When she wasn't fighting in bars, she was taking any sharp instrument she could find and slashing Carrie's arms. Wanda was simply unable to recognize that hurting Carrie was the same as hurting herself. She was consumed by hate, and such pure venom doesn't respond to logic or reason.

During this period Randolph Hornsby began considering divorce. Carrie no longer gave him any pleasure; she frightened him. If he was brutal to Carrie—and he enjoyed such violence—Wanda was likely to attack him, and she didn't care what she did to him. She would have killed him if he hadn't been able to flee the house at such times.

Randolph also found that the cost of Carrie's treatment was draining his income. He investigated getting help from welfare, especially since Carrie could no longer hold a steady job, but they would only help her if the couple was legally separated or divorced.

Randolph weighed the alternatives. He could live with a beautiful but totally unpredictable woman, paying for her medical care, or he could divorce her and let the state pick up the tab. He decided divorce was the only answer for him.

I was thrilled with Randolph's decision. He had a girl friend on the side and very conveniently moved in with her, leaving the house to Carrie. She was shocked by the action, depressed and bitter, but I knew that over the long haul she would be better off. Unfortunately, she was drinking heavily and I had to stay alert to potential suicide attempts.

My treatment plan for both Carrie and Janette was developing by trial and error. There was nothing to go on but guesswork, although the steps I took have proved workable, and I have successfully applied them to similar patients.

At the outset, I decided to concern myself only with the patient's major difficulties. I wanted to explore the circumstances surrounding the creation of each personality. At those times, physical flight had been impossible for the patient and mental escape, through the creation of an alter personality, was the only coping mechanism at her disposal. I felt that if I could uncover these occurrences, help the adult patient understand them, and find new ways to deal with such problems, the personalities would eventually fuse together into a whole individual who could function normally.

Such a statement about fusion sounds very calm and reasoned. However, at the time, there was absolutely nothing of value in the psychiatric literature concerning fusion. Again, I was pioneering new territory. I didn't know how to induce psychological health in a patient with such an extreme mental illness. I just had to assume that since the person had been able to cope only with the psychological crutch of an alter personality, the introduction of an alternative way of coping would be beneficial. My theories proved effective and other psychiatrists have adopted variations of them. Yet we still have no certain understanding of why the mind becomes whole after the patient learns to cope with past traumas in a new way.

This is one of the problems of psychiatry. There is so much we do not know about the mind, but our intellectual curiosity must be tempered by our primary job of helping the patient recover. Thus, things often happen during therapy for which we have no explanation. Fusion is a good example. Although we can lead patients to sound mental health, the reason our approach works often remains a mystery.

I had little time for intellectual speculation in those early years. My concern was with a person who was desperately in need of help and I had to do anything necessary to keep her alive until I could find a way to help her think constructively.

As Carrie's therapy progressed, I found myself resorting to the type of unorthodox procedure I'd first utilized in her "exorcism." Not surprisingly, such procedures often proved more useful, both in Carrie's case and in later cases, because multiple personality is such a complex problem and not easily resolved with "textbook" treatment.

My second venture into such unknown territory came about as a result of a new crisis in Carrie's life. The crisis arose by chance, brought on by Carrie's impending divorce and pressure she was feeling from both myself and her father.

After Randolph moved out, Carrie's father called her repeatedly to ask if she'd like to go sailing on a boat he owned. His motives were genuine—he wanted to help her through a particularly difficult period. Unfortunately, she was drinking heavily at the time and became abusive to him. Because he couldn't really understand what she was going through, he became angry in turn. He told her that if she couldn't respond graciously to his offer of help, she could go to hell for all he cared. He ended their conversation by telling her he no longer wanted anything to do with her.

About the same time, I got word that Carrie had been given a speeding ticket for going over ninety-nine miles an hour on the freeway and had narrowly missed colliding with a truck. This was one of a number of tickets she had gotten since I first started treating her, although this was the most serious. The recklessness of her actions put both herself and others on the road in serious danger. I informed her that she had to install a governor on the accelerator to control her speed or I would contact the authorities and have her license revoked. Despite her illness, Carrie was capable of driving safely, so in the past there had been no reason to inconvenience her by talking to the police. However, this latest ticket forced me to clamp down on her to insure that an innocent person didn't suffer from her recklessness on the road. Carrie responded to my actions, and her father's words, as an attack on her and her childish, irresponsible behavior. She felt she was being told to grow up "or else." The extreme emphasis on "or else" was her perception. We were actually just trying to teach her to act in a responsible manner for everyone's sake.

Although Carrie had begun to rely on the alter personalities less frequently, these pressures seemed to be too much. One evening her father received an hysterical telephone call from her. "I've got to grow up," she sobbed. "I've got to grow up." He couldn't hear anything else and he couldn't engage in more of a conversation.

The next day Carrie came to see me. But she herself wasn't there; "everyone" else was. She was switching personalities one after the other. Her face was like a flickering motion picture, the image changing constantly. I had no idea to whom I was talking. It could have been a familiar personality or someone new. There was no way of telling.

I asked Carrie a number of basic questions about herself and she couldn't answer them. She didn't know how to count. She couldn't add simple numbers. She couldn't name the alter personalities whom she had known for some time. She didn't know the names of the people in her family, where she lived, or anything else.

Carrie had a boyfriend at that point and I asked him to take her home and stay with her. I also alerted her parents to the situation. She needed help getting dressed, going to the bathroom, and handling all simple chores. It was a situation that frightened me greatly.

I had never read anything about an individual totally losing the ability to perform the most basic functions of life. To my knowledge, even now this situation is not covered in the psychiatric literature. Thus, I was again stepping into new territory with no idea how to handle the matter.

Fortunately, Carrie did not stay in such a state for very long. Her current boyfriend, someone she had been extremely close to in high school, agreed to come over and stay with her as much as possible during the coming week. He cared for her, talked to her, and helped her return to normal. She seemed to get better by the hour and after a week was functioning normally again. To this day, I can't explain what happened or why she recovered.

A couple of weeks later Carrie came to my office, extremely upset. "I can't sleep in my bedroom anymore," she told me. She was living in the house she had shared with Randolph before the divorce. There were two bedrooms on the first floor. She and her ex-husband had slept in the right bedroom; the left bedroom had been used as a spare. It also had a door leading to the fire escape. "Every time I go into my bedroom," she told me, "I hear a male voice telling me I'm going to die. The only way I can sleep without hearing the voice is to go in the other bedroom.

"But even that spare bedroom doesn't seem right. The doorknob keeps moving when nobody's around. I open it and check the fire escape, but nobody's there. I'll even look all around the house, in the bushes, everywhere somebody could hide, but nobody's out there. Yet the handle keeps moving.

"And the bathroom . . ." she continued, her voice rising in pitch. She seemed on the verge of hysteria. "I . . . I can't look in the mirror in the upstairs bathroom. When I do, I see myself lying in a coffin, dead. I don't see my reflection as I am. I see myself dead. I see myself . . . myself . . ." She began sobbing.

There are times when a psychiatrist feels absolutely helpless. The patient is obviously troubled, desperately in need of help, yet the problem he or she presents is so complex that it seems to defy solution. This was the case with Carrie.

I calmed her, using whatever psychiatric mumbo jumbo seemed soothing. One advantage about my profession is the language. It is so complex, and the jargon so confusing, even to other psychiatrists, that you can say nothing and sound very learned. Whatever nonsense I spouted apparently gave her confidence in my ability to solve this new problem. She left happily and I had time to think before seeing my next patient.

Later that afternoon I talked with another doctor and we went over all the possible causes of Carrie's problem. Neither of us knew what to do, although I sensibly decided to visit the house and observe it myself.

For the next couple of days, I thought constantly about what I would do when I reached Carrie's house, yet answers eluded me. I mentally reviewed some of her personalities, finally deciding that whatever was happening probably related to the evil personality, Wanda, the violent alcoholic. But what to do . . . What to do . . .

On Saturday I went to my office before visiting Carrie, and I happened to glance at my desk. Earlier in the week I had received a paperweight as a promotional gift from a pharmaceutical company. It was shaped like a giant tranquilizer pill, hardly something I needed, but because I am the kind of pack rat who hates to throw anything away, I had left it on my desk. For no conscious reason I stuck it in my pocket. Maybe I'll give it to Wanda, I thought to myself, smiling, a giant pill for a giant "pill."

My mind has always worked on two different levels. There are my conscious actions, those carefully reasoned, well-thought-out decisions based solely on experience and learning. Then there are my unconscious actions, the things I do because they "feel" right to me. It was this unconscious side which was to control my following actions. Even today, I can find no other explanation.

Carrie showed me the bedroom where all the problems were occurring. She stayed well away from the entrance while I went inside. She was still quite upset, although she expressed relief that I was present.

I walked over to the edge of the bed, sat down, and closed my eyes. I tried to block all thoughts and emotions from my mind except those that related to my surroundings. I focused my attention on the room, trying to feel whatever it was that Carrie had experienced. I didn't know what I hoped to learn, but it seemed worth trying.

Suddenly I became quite upset; I could sense the presence of something wrong in the room. I shuddered, not knowing whether the room really was "evil" or if I had just let my imagination get the best of me. Perhaps it was simply that Carrie was so frightened her terror had influenced me.

I left the bedroom and looked in the bathroom mirror. All I saw was my reflection, although I realized that this was the bathroom where Wanda had slashed her wrists several times in the past.

Suddenly one possible explanation became clear to me. Carrie was having experiences in rooms where extremely unpleasant events had taken place. Wanda was frequently in the bathroom, for example, but always to take pills or grab a razor in order to do violence to the shared body.

The bedroom was the one in which Randolph had made love to Carrie. But their love-making was not normal. He became aroused by seeing her experience pain. He would use all kinds of devices to hurt her, often pushing objects into her vagina. It was no wonder that she felt so uneasy in a room where so many awful things had occurred.

Carrie came to the bathroom and I had her sit on the closed toilet seat. Then I proceeded to talk to Wanda as though she could hear me. I did not call her out because I did not want her in control of Carrie's body. But I did speak to her, saying, "Wanda, your time has come! I'm going to get rid of you, Wanda. You have been torturing Carrie long enough. You're going to go from here!"

Wanda was created to express the anger and hostility that Carrie could not handle. If Carrie had let herself become angry under normal circumstances, there would have been no need for Wanda. But Carrie had never been able to tell anyone that their actions upset her. Outwardly, she accepted everything anyone did, inwardly building anger and hostility until it overwhelmed her and Wanda came forth to express it.

Anger and hostility are like quantities of energy stored in a container of limited capacity. There is a point at which it all overflows and that is when Wanda would take command. I figured that if I could somehow force Carrie to bring forth this angry energy, she could reduce Wanda's strength and perhaps learn to cope without resorting to her alter personalities.

Multiple-personality patients have excellent imaginations. They can take word imagery and use it to create reality in their minds. Symbolism is important to them. Thus, I decided to combine these elements of Carrie's personality to eliminate her fears.

I don't remember exactly what I said. I was dealing with a

crisis situation and I had to work quickly because Carrie had difficulty concentrating on my words. As I became more experienced with such patients, I refined and developed a similar routine for regular use. It is more involved and requires the patient to concentrate intensely, so I use it primarily in my office or at the hospital, where the surroundings are usually more tranquil.

At that moment, however, I instinctively grabbed the large paperweight and held it against Carrie's palm. We were palm to palm, the paperweight between our hands, as she sat on the closed toilet seat. I told her to push Wanda's anger from her body into the paperweight. I told her to take the anger from her head, her arms, her legs, and all the other parts of her body, as well as from the floor, walls, and ceiling of the bathroom. I wanted her to eliminate every perception of Wanda's strong emotionalism. I mentioned all the items I could see in the bathroom, including towels, soap, and even her toothbrush. Anything Carrie had used, Wanda undoubtedly had also used.

I had no idea whether or not Wanda's presence actually permeated the physical objects in the room. However, I was certain that Carrie believed in her angry alter personality's overriding presence and I needed to work within her belief system.

Carrie began twisting and turning her body, moaning, groaning, and straining. She writhed and pushed in a genuine attempt to rid her body of the evil personified by Wanda. As she pushed into the "pill," I told her that she would be perfectly able to get angry in the future. However, instead of storing it until it overwhelmed her, she would express it immediately.

Then Carrie was through. Her body relaxed and she slumped forward, forcing me to catch her so she wouldn't hit her head against the floor. In a moment she had recovered and was sitting upright, her face relaxed, her body free of tension. She was smiling and happy. She looked in the mirror and told me that she saw nothing but the reflection of her own face. There was no more coffin with its "dead" Carrie.

I decided to carry my symbolism a bit further. I took the

pill/paperweight, and Carrie and I walked to the river, a distance of a little more than a block from her home. Then I hurled the paperweight into the water, symbolically destroying Wanda.

When we returned to the house, we went to the bedroom to see how Carrie felt about that room. She was less uneasy, but felt there was still tension in it. We decided to perform a similar rite.

I looked around the room, trying to find something symbolic to use while Carrie told me more about the kind of sexual violence her husband had enjoyed. He had liked to stick objects up her rear end, but she would not be more specific except to describe the pain and humiliation she had felt at those times.

In light of these awful memories, I felt the symbolism should represent sadomasochistic sex. I grabbed a glass ashtray and told Carrie that it represented a woman's vagina since it was concave. The groove used to hold a cigarette represented the erect penis. I told her the burning end of the cigarette was the pain of the sadistic treatment she had endured.

I set the ashtray on the bed and told Carrie that she was going to become a magnet for all the bad vibrations filling the room. All the violence and pain would be drawn into her body. Then we followed the same routine we had used in the bathroom, driving this evil into the ashtray. It took about two minutes and when it was over, she announced that she was exhausted.

As soon as I left, pocketing the ashtray to carry the "evil" presence away, Carrie went into the bedroom and went to sleep. It was the first time in two weeks she could remain in that room without experiencing terror. In fact, she later told me that she had slept like a baby. I proceeded to drive by the town dump to toss the ashtray in a rubbish heap before going back to the office. No sense in taking any chances.

When I returned to the office, I thought about what I had done. If anyone had told me when I started medical school that I would one day encourage patients to push "evil energy" into a paperweight, I would have thought the person was crazy. I wasn't even certain I believed what had happened; I had no idea whether or not "evil energy" really does exist. I only knew that my imagery hit a responsive chord in Carrie and that my action brought her peace.

I thought about contacting other psychiatrists to find out if they had ever used such unusual methods. I wanted to know I wasn't the only one, that other doctors had risked making fools of themselves on a patient's behalf. However, I never had the courage to act on my desire. I was afraid I would be ridiculed and drummed from the ranks of the American Psychiatric Association.

Never again, I vowed. No way was I going to repeat such a stunt. And yet I had crossed the line between psychiatry practiced for peer approval and psychiatry practiced for the benefit of the patient. At that moment I knew I would always follow my instincts and experiences rather than a textbook whose writer had never faced my particular patient.

Did it really matter if anyone observing what I had done with Carrie thought I was crazy? Of course not. What I did seemed right to me at the time because it had a positive effect on my patient. Her fears and hallucinations vanished. I knew I hadn't rid her of Wanda. Carrie still needed to learn how to cope without the crutch of alter personalities. But she was stronger, happier, and more relaxed, all necessary steps toward her eventual recovery. She could relate to the experience in a positive way. It had been beneficial.

To hell with orthodoxy. From that moment forward I decided that I would do whatever I thought might work to help a patient. If it was something no one had ever recorded in the literature studied in medical school, it didn't matter. The patient was the target of my work; the patient's mental health, the goal of my efforts. If I could help a troubled mind accept reality, know joy, love, friendship, and the beauty of life, then whatever I did was "right."

My stand has often left me at odds with colleagues, but I have continued to try the unusual when necessary. My patients' welfare is the only consideration, and I will match my success rate with anyone's.

I don't always like being a loner. It hurts to know that I am ridiculed as a "fool" by people who don't dispute my successes, only my methods. At times I would certainly like the acclaim that I might receive were my methods more "traditional." But even more, I want my patients to get well as quickly as possible. And sometimes, especially with multiple-personality cases, that means rejecting orthodoxy for whatever works at a particular moment for a particular patient.

Every day with a multiple-personality patient is a surprise. Sometimes the situations can be humorous; at other times they are tragic. One of the most painful lessons Carrie taught me was just how strong a multiple-personality patient can be. She didn't weigh much more than 100 pounds; her body was thin and lacked muscles. Anyone could have overpowered her with very little force. At least that was true when she was herself.

The violent incident occurred near the end of Carrie's life. She was working and remarried, this time to a penniless alcoholic she had met at an alcoholic treatment center where she was a nurse. He was a psychopath who had been kicked out of every alcoholic treatment center in the community because he had tried to stay on a continuous drunk for the past five years. The hospital where Carrie worked would be his last because he had run out of money. Marrying Carrie seemed to be the answer to all his problems; he would be supported by someone who wouldn't mind his drinking. Needless to say, the wedding did not have my blessing, a fact neither of them cared about.

The marriage was a disaster from the start. The couple fought, drank too much, and went into debt. To his credit, Carrie's husband suggested that perhaps they had made a mistake. However, instead of agreeing to this obvious fact, she blew up at him and he reluctantly agreed to continue to try to make things work.

One afternoon I received a call from Carrie's husband. He said that Carrie had blown up at him for no reason after returning from her sister's house. She was acting so strangely that he wondered if I could come over to evaluate Carrie and help him deal with the problem. Since I had some free time, I drove over to their apartment, where they were in the midst of unloading groceries from the car.

"Dr. Allison," Carrie said, "how nice to see you. Were you just passing by or did you come for a reason?"

She was charming, calm, and in complete control. I couldn't understand what her husband had meant. When I was invited inside, I accompanied them into the kitchen. Carrie put down the groceries, smiling happily.

Suddenly Carrie turned, her face hard, her eyes glaring. "GoddamnmotherfuckingbastardIhateyou," she screamed, her words running together, her harsh voice echoing from the walls. She ran toward me, flailing her fists against my body. The blows were hard, almost like a boxer's, and I seriously feared that she might kill me.

I curled my body, bringing my arms up to ward off the blows. Then I reached out, grabbing for her wrists. Her fists struck my neck and groin. The pain rushed through my body. I feared I would lose consciousness and that she might kick me to death before her husband could get her off me. Desperately, I held her, ignoring the way she repeatedly brought her knee into my stomach and genitals.

Carrie twisted and turned in my grasp. Her arms were like steel and she jerked them away from my control. Then she ran into the bathroom, stopped, turned around, and came out.

"Hi, Dr. Allison," said the woman in front of me. "Boy, she sure got mad at you, didn't she?" She giggled, shrugged her shoulders, and looked up at me rather sheepishly. "I hope she didn't hurt you. It took me awhile to get her controlled."

"Debra?" I asked. "Is that you?"

"Of course," she giggled. "And I'm really sorry about the way she behaved. I—"

"YougoddamnmotherfuckingsonofabitchI'mgonna . . ." screamed the person I had seen before. She rushed at me again and this time her husband tackled her. As she fell forward, I wrapped my arms around her and together we held her down. I was double her weight and her husband was fairly large too, yet it was all I could do to keep her under control while I tried to telephone the police and arrange for some officers and an ambulance to come out.

When the officers arrived, I was barely able to open the door for them. They saw Carrie's husband and me struggling with this small, beautiful woman and asked me what was wrong. As I started to explain, I felt her body go limp and heard giggling again.

"You can let go now, Dr. Allison. It's me, Debra. Are those real policemen? Are we going to ride in the police car? I've always wanted to see a real police station." She giggled again.

I explained the situation to the four police officers, although I was certain they didn't believe a word I had to say. Fortunately, they had had to arrest Carrie before when she made scenes in bars and other public places so they assumed that there was a chance I was right. Still, it looked fairly strange to see her husband, four burly police officers, and me escort this frail beauty as she skipped to the ambulance.

"Can I ride in there? Are you going to play the siren? Are you—"

"CocksuckingpigsI'mnotgoinganywherewithyoumother . . ." The other woman had returned. She kicked one police officer in the groin, then stamped on the foot of a second, smashing his toes. She swung at the neck of the third and suddenly there was a free-for-all, with four police officers, two ambulance attendants, her husband, and me barely able to contain her. After several minutes, she was handcuffed and strapped to the stretcher, where she lay writhing and screaming all the way to the hospital.

I never did find out who the woman was. At the time of the incident, most of Carrie's personalities had been integrated and she was close to a cure. I suspect that she had let her anger with her new husband build internally. She didn't want to admit that she had made a mistake. She didn't want to complain to me or discuss the habits she disliked with him. Instead, she suppressed all her feelings until it was impossible to contain them. Since she refused to cope in a healthy manner, she handled the problem the way she had all her life. She created a new, ultraviolent personality. I was sure it wasn't Wanda, since Wanda had been gone for a while and had never been so insanely violent toward others. This was definitely someone new and I hoped I would never see that personality again.

The next day I went to see Carrie in the hospital. She had total amnesia about everything that had happened from the time she had left her sister's house until she awakened at 8 A.M. the next morning in the hospital seclusion room. She was quite embarrassed and upset when I filled her in on the details. She was not proud of what she had done, and she was very worried that I would think badly of her.

I tried to calm Carrie and explain that I wasn't angry at her. I thought I made it clear that I cared deeply about her and was very anxious that she get well. Perhaps I did. Perhaps that wasn't enough. Perhaps her emotional problems were so overwhelming that even the knowledge of other people's love and concern meant nothing. I don't know.

When Carrie was discharged, she went home to her "stash." She frequently used sleeping medicine legitimately prescribed for her and had apparently saved some of the pills from each refill. She had also accumulated drug samples left for the doctor she worked for.

How does a psychiatrist face the loss of a patient? I don't know how others do it. It is a subject none of us wants to face or discuss. Yet death is part of our practice. And when death comes, the shock can be devastating.

For me, Carrie's death brought a soul-searching reevaluation of who I was and where I was going. It was the most painful experience I have ever endured and I wish to God I had been alert enough to prevent the suicide. But I still had others who needed me. Janette remained in treatment and I had to find ways to keep her going until she could cope on her own. I moved forward, older, sadder, with an ache in my heart that diminishes with time but will never fully disappear.

Carrie's case forced me to confront issues in my professional life and helped me to become more responsive to the individual needs of my patients. She taught me to remain open to the exploration of unknown avenues of the mind, and she introduced me to the concept of parapsychology in my psychiatric practice. For the first time I faced circumstances that could not be explained by current psychological knowledge. The presence of Bonnie, the idea of spirit possession, is a concept that does not fit into the neat categories defined by Freud, Jung, and other pioneers of psychiatry. I came to see that no matter what I *knew,* my patients had experiences that defied both logic and traditional thinking. Yet I had to face these experiences and deal with them in an effective manner. I would have to remain open to these new concepts.

I hoped that I would never encounter another Carrie or Janette, yet I felt that since two such cases had occurred in my practice, it was likely that there were many more in the world than anyone realized. Perhaps the only reason they were rare was because other psychiatrists had closed their minds to the possibility.

And so I continued with my practice. I sometimes felt I was just going through the motions, especially in the first days after Carrie's death. Then I began to move forward, functioning effectively once again. I accepted the fact that Janette chose to live and Carrie chose to die. I could never turn back the clock, although I would try to make certain such a loss never happened again.

Chapter 4

My Search for the Inner Workings of the Mind

Shortly after Carrie's death, Janette moved away. My experiences with both women had had a profound effect on me and I felt their absence keenly. Although my treatment of Janette had been successful, I had to face the fact that I'd been unable to help Carrie find a reason for living. Yet I knew I had done everything possible. The real problem was the total lack of knowledge about this strange illness. I realized anew that I was a student of the mind, not its master. I vowed to continue my study of the human mind so that I could, if necessary, prevent another needless suicide and help others like Carrie and Janette to live a normal life.

At the same time, I felt a tremendous sense of pride in what I'd already learned. I was formulating theories about the causes and treatment of multiple personality that were not a part of the psychiatric literature. I had amassed information about aspects of the mind which would offer others a new understanding of certain psychological processes. I had, in effect, become a pioneer, and I was pleased with my new role. I had always assumed that as a small-town doctor I would never make the kind of unique discoveries that originate from major universities and medical teaching centers. Yet I had, to the best of my knowledge, developed new techniques, and I was anxious to share my information with my colleagues.

I have always believed that it is absolutely vital for the medical community to pool all resources and information. Perhaps another doctor would want to try an approach similar to mine. So I began writing articles in various medical journals about multiple personality, emphasizing what I had encountered, how I'd handled it and what the results were.

I was also encountering new cases of this unusual illness. This doesn't mean that I suddenly came to the conclusion that all my patients were multiple personalities. Rather, I accepted the premise that this illness was more prevalent than I had realized in the past. Thus, I felt that my expanding knowledge of multiple personality would be of interest to other doctors.

It is hard to say why I assumed there would be broad general interest in my findings. Locally, I was having some problems. Other psychiatrists had to interact with my patients from time to time when my patients were in the hospital. The multiple personalities I had uncovered were often demanding, unpleasant, and a tremendous emotional drain. They required an unusual amount of patience. Some of my colleagues, viewing my patients in the halls on a casual basis, saw them as thoroughly unpleasant people without analyzing the cause. After all, the patients weren't in treatment with them. The other psychiatrists did not have to control their feelings since there was no patient-therapist interaction between them and my hospitalized patients.

So my decision to publicize my work created unexpected problems for me. During this same period, the concept of peer review developed in California. The state government felt that doctors had too much power; they were answerable to no one and could easily abuse their power. Because medicine is such a specialized field, it is impossible for either patients or laymen to question a doctor's judgment, so it fell to other doctors to assume this responsibility. Doctors began reviewing one another's work in order to abolish various abuses that might go unnoticed by the patient.

Because state officials were worried about the real or potential abuse of unnecessary hospitalization, the various state and county psychiatric associations were asked to develop a prevention plan. The alternative was government intervention and control, since hospital utilization was a major cost factor for insurance companies. Consequently, psychiatric peer review developed through the Medicare and Medi-Cal programs.

When peer review was introduced, I was associated with a small 150-bed general hospital that contained a 12-bed psychiatric ward. Although a number of doctors were free to use the ward, six of us utilized the space on a fairly regular basis.

The number of psychiatrists involved in the ward posed additional problems in terms of peer review. In the Community Mental Health Service hospital, the psychiatric ward was run by one full-time resident who established a uniform treatment program for all patients. Peer review in such a situation is relatively simple since a patient's progress can be monitored by one measurable standard.

In contrast, peer review at our hospital was more difficult. Each psychiatrist had his own particular approach to treatment, and conflicts often arose between doctors. The patients fueled such conflicts by arguing among themselves about their different doctors and downgrading the treatment plans of any doctor other than their own. They complained to their psychiatrist about their feuds with other patients, and the doctors often became involved, criticizing their colleagues. It is an unfortunate and often childish situation, but we psychiatrists *are* human.

To solve this problem, we all voted together to establish standards for peer review. We worked on two major areas—utilization review and quality review. Utilization review involved the evaluation of measurable factors such as the duration of hospitalization. Quality review is an evaluation of clinical judgment.

In setting standards for utilization review, we were guided by the national statistics for length of stay in hospitals all over the country. In California, for example, most patients were grouped by type of illness; schizophrenics and manic-depressives were the two common categories. For these categories there was a fairly average treatment duration. Schizophrenics, for example, generally spent no more than one week in the type of general community hospital in which I practiced.

Actually, that statistic is misleading and must be viewed in light of professional knowledge. Schizophrenia is a long-term illness and patients are often hospitalized for months or years. However the initial testing period generally takes no more than a week, and that was enough to establish such a national average. After testing, patients are generally placed in a long-term mental health care facility, so the total treatment time is far in excess of the time spent in the general community hospital setting.

In our particular hospital, three fourths of all our psychiatric patients, regardless of their particular problem, were normally discharged within two weeks. Therefore, we felt that a two-week maximum stay would be acceptable under normal circumstances. If a patient's stay exceeded that limit, the doctor in charge might be faced with utilization review.

The review, however, was not a threatening procedure. The doctor in question had to justify a longer stay by explaining the patient's problem and his treatment approach. The validity of his approach was not in question; that was the province of quality review. If the doctor had a plan and a logical reason for such an extended-care situation, the review was over. It was only necessary to make sure the doctor wasn't abusing the hospitalization process in any way.

Utilization review can also help weed out lazy, disinterested, or incompetent psychiatrists. Occasionally a patient is admitted and left to languish without therapy, either because the doctor hasn't formulated a treatment plan or because he just doesn't care. The patient usually asks to go home when boredom sets in and leaves the hospital in much the same condition as when he arrived.

Although I acknowledged the importance of peer review, I did find the idea a little unsettling. I had enough confidence in my own decisions and ability, but I felt the concept was a difficult one to apply to the inexact science of psychiatry.

The establishment of peer review coincided with the publication of several of my articles on multiple personality. At the same time, I'd begun discussing my work with other psychiatrists in the community.

Their reactions were interesting, but occasionally negative. The worst came from another psychiatrist in my community who was one of several psychiatrists connected with the hospital. His actions toward me were so extremely hostile that even today it is hard for me to think about the man objectively.

On the telephone he told me that he could not handle his own uncomfortable feelings about my "strange" patients. Instead of attacking the patients, which he felt like doing, he attacked me, first by expressing doubt about the diagnosis, then by criticizing the novelty of my treatment methods. To make matters worse, he was the chairman of the department of psychiatry at that time and the head of the peer review committee.

Unfortunately, my multiple-personality patients often needed to be hospitalized for longer than two weeks, especially when I was taking them through the last stages of therapy prior to fusion. When he learned that one of my multiples was in for an extended stay, he insisted the patient be discharged at the end of the two-week period. He did not check my charts or talk to the patient in question. Nor did he ask me about my treatment plan. I would have welcomed any of these actions. Instead, he made up his mind to enforce the duration rule rigorously before hearing my side of the story.

In effect, this psychiatrist was fighting my work and challenging the quality of my care. He was questioning both the diagnosis and treatment of my patients. Yet he never admitted this publicly, and he never discussed the matter with me. He simply fought me without actual confrontation, and did not make the effort truly to investigate my work. To fight such a situation openly would only have caused more problems in a community as small as Santa Cruz.

In retrospect, the entire matter seems petty and unbecoming to professionals. Yet doctors participate in as much political backbiting and hostility as members of other professions.

The hospital utilization review process degenerated into an improper quality review in my case, which brought me under great pressure. In addition, I had discussed the exorcism I'd performed on Carrie during a meeting of one of the psychiatric associations. I presented it in a way that would not challenge the religious attitudes and biases of those present. I discussed all the symptoms exhibited and the belief system of the patient. Then I explained how I had worked within this belief system by performing the exorcism. I did not contend that I had actually rid the patient of evil spirits or even that the patient was possessed. I felt the successful result of the procedure would speak for itself. This was the scientifically proper way to introduce new concepts. Unfortunately, this brought even more criticism.

Many of my colleagues were unable to understand my actions in Carrie's case. The fact that I had not only accepted a patient's illogical belief, but had gone so far as to perform an exorcism seemed wrong and unprofessional to them. Many psychiatrists believe it is the doctor's responsibility to utilize logic to disprove a patient's irrational beliefs. They choose to ignore the patient's values if these appear beyond the range of acceptable scientific knowledge. The fact that I'd achieved such stunning results in only a few minutes didn't sway their judgment. They felt I should have systematically proved to Carrie that spirit possession was an impossibility, even if that took months of additional therapy. Such unreasonable, narrow attitudes are difficult to fight. I could not change what I had done, nor would I want to. And I was unable to explain myself in any way that they could understand. We had reached an impasse. Although their criticism hurt me, I continued to do what I thought was right.

Actually, quality review almost occurred in my case. My nemesis wanted to restrict my privileges at the hospital, although his reasons were never openly expressed. I could have been barred from bringing patients to the hospital or forced to admit them under some one else's direct care, thus diminishing my effectiveness as a doctor.

Proper quality review would have required the committee to study my patients' charts carefully, talk to the nurses I worked with, and perhaps interview the patients to determine their own independent diagnoses. However, none of this was done in my case. Fortunately, the hospital staff involved recognized the kangaroo court aspects of the charges, and the challenge to my privileges was dropped.

Although I had "won" my case, the pressure put a strain on my work and my personal life. My wife was hurt by the occasional nasty remarks she heard from the wives and office staff members of those doctors who disagreed with my approach.

For a while I seriously considered giving up my work with

multiple-personality patients. I could have simply ignored the possibility of multiple personality altogether, as some of my colleagues continued to do. That would have solved my personal problems, although it would have been a grave disservice to my patients. I also could have referred my multiple-personality patients to other doctors, which would have eased my conscience to some degree.

The options were many and I almost convinced myself to use them. The pressure was intense and my life would be a great deal simpler. Unfortunately, there were two strong reasons for continuing with my work. One was the intellectual curiosity I had developed about the illness. It fascinated me and I wanted to increase my knowledge of the causes, diagnosis, and treatment of multiple personality.

The second reason was one I didn't like to admit because it was purely emotional. I had been the direct or indirect cause of several deaths during my days of learning. The knowledge I had gained about multiple personality had come at the expense of at least one life already. I knew from the number of cases reported in the literature that I was conceivably one of the few doctors in the country dealing with this phenomenon. I was certainly the only one in my area and in much of the section of California my patients were from. Quite possibly there was no other place for these patients to go. Thus, I found myself almost trapped, if only by default, into feeling that I might be their last hope. I could not stop what I was doing and still live with myself.

Once I was able to stop feeling sorry for myself and return to the work at hand, I began analyzing what I knew about multiple-personality cases. They were not as unique as I had first supposed. There were certain shared experiences regardless of the differences in their backgrounds. For example, most experienced early, unpleasant, often abusive sex; a feeling of abandonment by the parent they perceived as being loving; and a sense of rejection by the other parent. These traumas were often coupled with child abuse and a real or imagined isolation from others. The exact circumstances differed in each case, of course. One girl was raped by her father, another by a stepfather, a third by a motorcycle gang, and a fourth by a schoolyard bully. Some were unwanted by both parents. Some were unable to differentiate between right and wrong. But in general, all multiple-personality patients seemed to share a number of childhood traumas. What was different was the strange yet fascinating way their cases unfolded and the kind of treatment I found myself using.

With each new multiple-personality patient, my body of knowledge grew. Yet it was difficult to formulate one general method of treatment since each patient responded in different ways. Procedures that worked in one case often failed in another, and I faced a constant challenge in devising an appropriate treatment.

All multiple-personality patients have an original or basic personality that emerges at birth. This personality, actually a collection of thoughts, memories, and behavior patterns, develops and changes as a result of the child's experiences. In normal people, this personality remains whole and defines them and contributes to their uniqueness. In multiple personalities, this original personality splinters into others.

Too little is known about multiple personality to predict with any certainty the range and diversity of alter personalities that any given person might develop. However, there are a number of consistent types that regularly emerge. Among these is the negative or persecutor alter personality who is created from the lower unconscious and generally negative forces within the individual. This is usually a destructive personality who engages in excessive drug abuse, exhibits violent behavior, and often puts the body in danger of injury or death. Some persecutor personalities claim that they follow Satan as a way of rejecting the main personality's belief in God. The negative personality's emotional energies are grounded in hatred, guilt, and fear. When Janette became angry, for example, and refused to express it, this anger would build and explode outwardly in the guise of her negative alter personality.

The positive rescuer or helper personality is an alter personality created from the upper unconscious forces, usually as a means of countering the negative alter personality. If the negative personality slashes the wrists, the rescuer might telephone for an ambulance. The rescuer wants to help the main personality survive, function effectively, and heal. It considers its existence temporary, knowing that it will fuse with the main personality when the person can function normally. Many rescuer personalities state that their ultimate allegiance is to God.

The Inner Self, separate from the conscious and unconscious mind, is characterized by qualities of love, knowledge, and strength. I see it as that part of the mind through which God is revealed to the individual. It might be said to carry the "genetic material" of the personality, so that the basic personality is not a blank tablet on which life will make its mark. If you believe in the concept of reincarnation, as many of my patients do, then the Inner Self is that part of the individual which continues to exist after the death of the body and retains the individual's past life experiences. It is incapable of negative emotions like anger, fear, or guilt.

Finally, there is the Inner Self Helper, which I consider an entity rather than a true alter personality. The Inner Self Helper (ISH) is revealed in a number of ways; through visions, automatic writing, speech, and the presence of an inner voice. It attempts to guide the patient toward sound mental health. I have had conversations with the ISH aspect of my patients, and I've discovered that they regard themselves as agents of God, with the power to help the main personality. I have encountered as many as six different entities within one individual, each an ISH, and each with a clearly defined rank. The lowest-level ISH is the first to reveal itself during therapy and eventually fuses with the patient. Some of the higher-ranking ISHs never seem truly to fuse; they continue to exist as spiritual teachers of the main personality. They remain dissociated in the mind even after the person becomes whole again.

An Inner Self Personality has also appeared during the course of my treatment with some patients. This is a rescuer personality which appears to be the strongest and most active protector of the main personality. In conversations with Inner Self Personalities, I have learned that they are closely associated with, and often created by, the ISH. Sometimes they are re-created from past rescuer personalities or may be fabricated when needed by the ISH.

During therapy, the patient and I work toward positive

psychological personality fusion. This occurs when all the negative persecutor alter personalities have been "cast out." The methods of achieving this vary from patient to patient, but it is a necessary step in the treatment process. Then, as the patient learns to assume the functions of the various remaining positive alter personalities, they are gradually merged until only a single personality and the ISH are left.

The final step before total recovery is positive spiritual fusion. This occurs between the final resulting personality and the ISH. It can happen so quietly that the patient remains almost unaware of the fusion, or the patient may experience either a vision or a strong sense of spirituality. Many patients have said that it occurs with a conscious determination to follow God as they understand Him.

Negative personality fusion is something no psychiatrist wants to consider, although it is a possibility we must all face. It would occur if the patient's main personality decided to yield to the negative personalities. The positive personalities would be expelled and the negative personalities would fuse.

Negative spiritual fusion would occur after negative personality fusion and would involve the complete destruction of the ISH. Such a person would be totally without conscience or moral judgment, and would be capable of committing any crime. If this has ever happened, it has not been within my experience.

Thus, positive spiritual fusion was my goal for each patient, and I found the Inner Self Helper a consistently useful therapeutic tool in achieving such fusion. Janette had first introduced me to the ISH, but Babs taught me just how important this entity can be. In fact, it can be a major factor in a patient's eventual recovery, and this was especially true in Babs's case.

Babs became my patient in 1973 after she was hospitalized for taking an overdose of barbiturates. She was in her early twenties and grotesquely fat. She was very short, yet weighed close to 300 pounds, and the folds of her fat almost hid the features of her face. She had a history of severe headaches and a number of emotional problems apparently unconnected with her suicide attempt.

Her marriage was one such problem. Her husband, Phil, an

accountant, was extremely passive and quiet, with little drive or ambition. His only real interest in life was religion. Although he'd been raised as a Catholic, he was deeply involved with an evangelical Pentecostal group who practiced faith healing. Babs hated the church and resented his dedication to it.

Babs and Phil had two children, a three-year-old daughter, and an eighteen-month-old son. They had recently learned that the little girl was brain-damaged and would require special schooling. Apparently, this news was the trigger for Babs's suicide attempt.

When I visited Babs at the hospital, I realized that she believed that her problems were insurmountable. She could no longer cope and suicide seemed the only way out. Like many mentally ill patients, Babs viewed life in black or white—all situations were either good or bad. She was incapable of perceiving options or alternatives to her problems. She couldn't afford to place her daughter in an institution, yet she believed this was the only solution to the problem. Nor could she afford the biofeedback treatments recommended for her paralyzing headaches. She felt trapped and she responded to all attempts at help with overt hostility.

I managed to convince Babs to use the biofeedback machine in my office. The machine helps people learn to control bodily processes through special conditioning. Patients are taught to sense internal changes and control them. Many migraine sufferers are being helped in this manner, and I had hired and trained one of my patients to operate the machine during my office hours.

Lila, my biofeedback technician, came to me rather excitedly after Babs had had one of her sessions. According to Lila, Babs was not acting in her usual manner. She was extremely energetic, smiling, and happy. She had boldly announced that she had decided to go home, lock Babs in a closet, and kill her. She said a few other things, similar in nature, always referring to Babs as a third party.

"I think Babs has my illness, Dr. Allison," said the worried Lila. She herself was a multiple-personality patient but she had responded so well to treatment that she no longer switched personalities unexpectedly. I trusted her completely, and my secretary confirmed that Lila did an excellent job. There was every reason to trust her judgment when she said, "I'm almost certain Babs is switching personalities on me."

I immediately arranged an office visit for Babs and gave her a special psychological test that would provide more background on her mental state. I also talked to her husband, who described occasional experiences that fit the pattern of multiple personality.

Our next session was a real breakthrough. The test revealed hints of schizophrenia as well as the dissociative behavior which characterizes multiple-personality patients. After persistent questioning, Babs admitted that she experienced blackouts; she had, she said, "missed" an entire year of high school. When I put her under hypnosis, I met Alice, an alter personality.

Therapy proceeded slowly because Babs had difficulty trusting me. Apparently I reminded her of her father and she had hated him. She was very uncooperative during our early sessions and was able to talk about her problems and experiences only when Lila was present. Fortunately, Lila was very understanding and agreed to stay with Babs during our talks. With Lila's help, I was finally able to identify three personalities.

The main personality was Babs herself. She was extremely quiet, easily hurt, and frightened of others. She believed that she was extremely inadequate, especially in social situations, and she was terrified of large groups of any kind. She responded by remaining at home as much as possible.

Alice, the first alter personality I had met, was the personality capable of raising the children. She filled the mother role, went to social gatherings, and handled all functions that Babs couldn't cope with. Alice had taken over during Babs's and Phil's wedding ceremony. Alice was also an excellent artist while Babs was incapable of drawing a straight line with a ruler. Alice was Babs's helper or rescuer personality.

Lenore, on the other hand, was the negative or persecutor personality. She was hostile and vicious. She berated Babs constantly, telling her what a bad mother she was. She smashed dishes and tried to hurt Babs, cutting her arm or slashing the body with glass shards. Lenore first emerged during an office visit when I had put Babs in a trance. Babs suddenly covered her face with a shawl, and when I attempted to remove the shawl, the person underneath began cursing me. She hated me, Babs's husband, and just about everyone she met, including the other personalities who were really just aspects of herself.

Although I wasn't sure if Lenore and Alice were the only alter personalities, I had begun to hope so. Thus, I was surprised and disturbed when Babs arrived for a session with an unusual story. She had found herself down on the wharf talking to a fisherman. She had no memory of going to the wharf and was very surprised when the fisherman called her "Tammy." Under the circumstances, I had to assume that Tammy was probably a fourth personality. Fortunately, Tammy telephoned me shortly thereafter and arranged to come to the office.

The difference between Tammy and Babs was amazing. There was no way Tammy could reduce the physical size of the body, of course, so she was as fat as Babs. However, the grotesqueness had disappeared. Tammy seemed to float rather than walk. She had a delicacy of movement that belied her size. She was smiling, almost glowing, in love with life and the world in general. She was gentle and polite—the kind of woman who could charm anyone.

There were other contrasts as well. Babs hated religion because of her husband's overzealous dedication to it. Tammy, on the other hand, was quite comfortable with religion. She was also skilled in Scripture quotation, although she used it only when appropriate. She wasn't evangelical, nor did she lean toward a particular group, but rather accepted the concept of God's power as natural.

Tammy was self-confident, but had none of Lenore's aggressiveness or hostility. She spoke softly, distinctly, and positively, as though she knew that her statements and beliefs were right.

Tammy explained much of Babs's background. She told me that Babs had been conceived out of wedlock; her mother had married her father when she was six months pregnant. The father was angry about the pregnancy and tried to abort Babs. When that failed, he abandoned his wife and infant daughter, leaving his wife to fend for herself. She didn't seem to want her daughter either and left Babs in her own parents' care.

What was most interesting about Tammy was her desire to help me coordinate Babs's treatment program. She went so far as to write a letter to Babs after I had made the multiple-personality diagnosis. The letter was meant to help Babs adjust to the reality of her illness and accept the assistance of this Inner Self Helper. The letter, written in my presence in a handwriting radically different from that of Babs's, said, "Hi, there. I am here to say Hi. You better believe what is said. I'll not harm you if you will admit what is true. You must let me come out more often. Please accept me. I already help you with the kids [Babs's children]. You know this. I will cooperate with you. Be talking to you. Signed, Tammy."

At my request, Tammy then went home and wrote a history of Babs's entire life. Before presenting this material, I want to emphasize that most of these details were unknown to Babs. Some were the experiences of the other personalities. Other details had been repressed because they were unpleasant. Tammy, like all Inner Self Helpers, was the only aspect of Babs's mind capable, at that point, of presenting the entire history. Everyone else had a very one-sided, limited view.

Repeated experience has convinced me that all Inner Self Helpers have the ability to provide a complete overview of the individual's past. I don't know why this is true, but I've come to believe it implicitly. The various other personalities are unable to tell me about all facets of the person's life. What they do know is colored by their own attitudes and prejudices. And when I have been able to cross-check the ISH's details, they have always proved accurate.

Tammy wrote:

"This is the information you requested on Babs Mulvaney as I recall it or as the Holy Spirit leads me to tell you." The religious reference has been repeated many times by other Inner Self Helpers. I do not know how significant this may be or if it just reflects the interest of the original personality in religion. I can only say that it seems to be a part of all Inner Self Helpers.

Tammy continued:

Babs's mother, Lainie, married Vincent Caspin in 1946. Babs came in January, 1947. The pregnancy was difficult because Lainie was under intense psychological pressure. Lainie's parents were always telling her that she shouldn't have married Vincent. Vincent and his mother tried to give Lainie some drugs to cause a miscarriage. They also put marbles on the stairs to try and make Lainie fall.

Vincent was a disturbed person who had never cut the apron strings with his mother. Lainie called her own mother who brought her home, but her presence caused increased tension between Lainie's mother and stepfather. They reminded her of her mistake often.

The facts were related in a dry, straightforward manner. They were extremely detailed, a fact I wondered about until Tammy added:

"You might wonder why I tell you this part of Babs's life. It is important because tension and an unhappy pregnancy can be an influence on the fetus."

Tammy traced some of Babs's problems back to the womb, where Babs had had her first sense of being an unwanted child. It is impossible to judge whether this concept is plausible. Other patients of mine have talked about prebirth feelings and sensations, and some doctors speculate that we do have buried memories of the fetal stage. But I accepted Tammy's statement because, if nothing else, my patient obviously believed it.

"Babs was born in January of 1947," Tammy continued, always referring to Babs as another person. "Mr. Caspin wanted to see her but was not allowed to do so since it would cause problems. Then Babs came to live with her grandparents. Her grandmother was sick and her grandfather assumed the responsibility for Babs's care. Her basinet was placed by his bed since he had broken feet.

"Then, in 1947, Lainie met Albert Bridgeford who was divorced. She liked him and decided to go to Reno for a divorce. Lainie's parents didn't like him, especially Lainie's father, so tension increased in the family."

Notice how Tammy was able to relate events and emotions that theoretically would not have registered on the infant

Babs. It was as though Tammy had existed on a different plane since birth, observing life with an understanding far beyond the physical years of the body in which she was existing. This fact has reinforced my belief that the ISH is an entity rather than a personality. Since no scientific explanation is possible, I have come to accept the religious concept proposed by many of the ISHs as a viable alternative.

> *When Babs was nine months old, Lainie and Albert were married and Babs went to live with them. Lainie's parents never forgot this. Even though they have never mentioned this to Babs's parents, they have often reminded Babs that she was theirs. They often said, "We took care of you. They took you from us. We wanted to adopt you." So, as you can see, there was conflict in this area of Babs's life.*
>
> *When Babs was two, her dad adopted her. This made her happy.*
>
> *When they lived on Belknap Street, Babs liked the back yard and the green fence but she started to get lonely. This is when Tammy came. I made a good playmate.*

Babs, like many children, created an imaginary playmate, settling on her ISH by chance. However, this playmate became all too real, developing an identity separate from that of Babs.

> *During this time Lainie had a few miscarriages and was very depressed. Then she got pregnant with Joan and had a difficult pregnancy. Babs secretly wished that something would happen to it. When Babs was four and one half, Joan was born.*
>
> *Joan had severely clubbed feet and a stomach condition so she was often sick. Babs felt very guilty about this—as if she were responsible.*
>
> *Babs was at Mirror Lake with her grandparents when Joan was born. When they came back to see Joan, her grandfather said, "Whoever gets to the door first gets to hold the baby first." He didn't realize it but he knocked into Babs, beating her to the door. This caused Lenore to make her first real appearance. Babs didn't know how to cope with her feelings of rejection and her hatred of Joan, so Lenore took care of it.*

It is difficult for a normal person to understand why such relatively minor childhood traumas would create multiple personality splits. However, in addition to the factors discussed in earlier chapters, all multiple-personality patients I have seen share an inability to learn from experience. They are unable to integrate daily experience into their general knowledge about life and the world around them.

The multiple-personality sufferer also seems to be in a moral limbo. Such a person straddles the fence on all issues, unwilling or unable to decide what is good and bad. In addition, the person usually has an especially sensitive nervous system and is extremely influenced by the emotional feelings and reactions of others.

In Babs's case, her extreme sensitivity plus her adoption of a kind of mental fleeing as a coping mechanism made it easy for Babs to split again. Each time she faced an emotional hurt or a problem that created unusual pressure for her, the creation of an alter personality to handle the matter became the method of choice for coping.

"It was during this time that Tammy came into action because of Lenore. Lenore often tried to hit or throw some object at Joan while Lainie wasn't looking. Tammy stopped her many times.

"When Joan was fifteen months old, she went to the hospital for surgery on her feet. When she returned home after Christmas they had a late celebration for her." Tammy explained that Babs became jealous when her parents gave Joan a rabbit. She took it and played with it and Joan began crying. When that happened, her parents made Babs return it. Babs realized that she could get her way by becoming a "baby" like Joan, so Sandra was created. Sandra kept her thumb in her mouth and cried often, every inch the child Babs perceived Joan to be.

Sandra was another personality who played a relatively minor role in Babs's life. Sandra was always an infant, using a baby's behavior to get her way. Tammy made it clear that Sandra was created in imitation of the real baby, Joan, of whom Babs was jealous. It was a way of getting the attention she craved.

"When Babs was four and a half she started kindergarten,

which she liked. Her teacher, Mrs. Williams, gave Babs much love, but in first grade, Babs was placed in Mrs. Saunders's class. She also had two other teachers during this period, but none of them realized they each had four different people in their class—Babs, Tammy, Lenore and Sandra."

Tammy then talked about an aunt who sexually manipulated Babs:

> *There was an Aunt Carmen who came down to Babs's grandparents' house. Babs hated her. She used to take Babs into the bedroom in the small house and play nurse with her. She would make Babs take the tweezers and pull the hair from her arms and legs. [This aunt also made Babs brush the hair between the woman's legs, giving Carmen sexual pleasure that Babs knew was wrong, although she didn't know why.]*
>
> *Sandra would come out and cry when the aunt made Babs play nurse. Then the aunt would take Sandra and touch her breasts to Sandra's face and make her touch them. When no one was around, Aunt Carmen would undress Babs and touch her and place Babs on her body, rubbing Babs against her and sometimes touching her private parts.*
>
> *When this happened, either Sandra or Lenore would come out. Lenore once bit Aunt Carmen hard.*
>
> *Aunt Carmen made Babs promise never to tell anyone what happened—or else. To this day nobody knows or even suspects what took place. The memory of this experience has plagued Babs during her sexual experiences with her husband, Phil, so she lets Alice come out.*

Alice was a personality created when Babs was a teen-ager. Alice was a social being who could go to parties and church functions and otherwise engage in normal interaction with others without feeling guilty. Alice enjoyed sexual relations with Phil whenever Babs felt herself unable to handle the relationship.

> *In third grade, Babs had a teacher she hated. She also became interested in her first father and why he had left her. She loved her current father but was curious. When*

this curiosity was suppressed by her mother, Amy, a weak personality, was created.

In fourth grade, Babs's parents decided to move to another city and felt it best not to tell her. Babs found out about it at a Brownie meeting (from the child of a friend of the family who knew of the plans) and was really upset. Tammy had to make the trip to the new home.

Babs didn't like the new school and was teased by the other kids. She was behind in her studies so her parents had a tutor teach her the multiplication tables. Babs created a new personality, Candance, who did most of the learning.

During this same year, Babs's grandfather died from cancer. Her fear of death began at this time. She was old enough to see her grandfather's suffering. She saw him for the last time two days before he died and then was required to view the remains at the funeral.

Tammy was telling me Babs's entire life history, stressing each trauma that affected Babs. It would take years for a Freudian analyst to dig out this kind of crucial information. However, I had tapped into the Inner Self Helper, who laid everything at my feet. I knew at which ages she had faced problems that overwhelmed her. I would only have to take her back to these periods, help her understand them and find a new method for coping that would not involve splitting into separate personalities.

Tammy went on to describe an incident that happened when Babs was in junior high. She was returning home from baby-sitting when a man came up to her and sexually attacked her. She was saved only by the vicious Lenore. Since the man was drunk, Lenore threatened to tell the police. He gave her five dollars to keep quiet.

Babs discovered the five dollars in her purse when she returned home. She didn't know where the money had come from but was worried she might have done something wrong to have gotten it. She decided not to tell her father, fearing the possible consequences.

During these years, Babs spent a lot of time alone in her room listening to the radio. This is when Alice came.

Alice became the socializer. Alice and Candance spent more time at church-related gatherings than Babs, although Babs herself had first joined the social group. Candance received a standing ovation for her recital of the girls' club pledge.

Babs went to a beach party with the group and met a boy who asked her to go for a walk. Babs wasn't sure she should, but Lenore thought it would be fun and took control. He had a broken leg so they walked to the pier and sat down. He started to kiss her, then touch her, and finally he threw his cast-wrapped leg over her body. Lenore kicked and scratched him and took off. She went to the bathroom, then returned control of the body to Babs. Babs didn't know how she had gotten into the bathroom and had no idea about the incident on the pier. She just rejoined the party.

During this time, Babs became jealous of her sister. The sister always seemed to be in the limelight so Babs let Jo-Ann, a new personality, come out. Jo-Ann was really a take-off of Joan. She was hostile and walked with a bent foot. She could only shake her head "yes" and "no." This is also a weak personality.

Babs's mother was becoming more and more jealous of her husband. She thought he was out seeing other women and had fantasies about this. She was either manic-depressive or borderline schizophrenic. She was hospitalized three or four times for mental depression and had twenty-one shock treatments. She took tranquilizers and sometimes used alcohol to feel better, yet Babs's father refused to believe it. He blamed her mental illness on the accident and on the hysterectomy. During Babs's high school years, Lainie got much better.

While Babs's mother was sick, her dad didn't realize it and made some very bad remarks about his wife. These made a strong impression on Babs. Her father is well meaning but very stubborn and loves to argue. He'll never admit he is wrong.

After high school, Babs lived with her parents for a few months. Then her mother had a breakdown and her aunt decided it would be good for Babs to be a hairdresser. She was sent to beauty school.

After Babs got her beautician's license and went to live with her father's parents, her emotional problems became more severe. Alter personalities would take care of the customers, clean the shop, and handle other chores. Then Babs would find herself standing around with no idea which customers had been handled and what work was left to be done.

Her living situation was also difficult. Her grandparents fought constantly. Her grandfather always talked about sex and went so far as to proposition his granddaughter. He also accused her father of causing her mother's illness, thus tearing down one of the few people she loved.

Babs moved out on her own, but her fear was so great that Tammy had to take control in order to run the apartment. Alice took advantage of the place to begin dating heavily, and even Babs had a date with a boy who was serving in the Navy. As Tammy explained:

"He was a typical sailor. Babs got chicken because she realized he was a drug freak and she asked to be taken home. Before he could say anything, Alice came out and went to a party with him. It turned out to be a drug party. Alice smoked some grass and it made her feel good. Then Cliff [the boy in the Navy] tried to give her a drink but Tammy warned her that it could have LSD in it so she should be careful. When she turned it down, Cliff tried to force it down her throat so Lenore came out and made a scene, fleeing through the door. When she gave up control of the body, Babs found herself about four miles from her apartment at two in the morning. She didn't know what happened and walked home, feeling sick to her stomach."

In June of 1968, Babs met Phil, the accountant she eventually married. She fell in love with him and, in August, agreed to marry him. Alice was apparently thrilled with the idea, took control of the body, and went to bed with Phil. Babs found herself lying beside her naked fiancé at 3 A.M., knowing she had had sex with him but unable to remember any of it. Even more frightening to her was the fact that premarital sex violated her personal moral code. She was ashamed, yet pretended awareness when Phil discussed it with her.

Babs loved Phil, and she didn't realize the affection wasn't mutual. However, when they took premarital counseling with the minister who eventually married them, Phil said that he was marrying Babs for companionship. She was overwhelmed and Alice had to take over. In fact, after the marriage, Babs couldn't bring herself to have sex with a man who didn't love her, so Alice always went to bed with him. To his credit, Phil eventually came to love Babs as much as she had first hoped.

Babs had one miscarriage, then gave birth to an epileptic daughter. She blamed herself and became very depressed.

The next pregnancy was a difficult one and the doctor assumed the baby would be born dead. Babs was convinced she was carrying the son her husband wanted and she was determined he would be born healthy. She prayed constantly and, despite an extremely difficult delivery, the baby boy was healthy.

The intense pain of delivery brought Lenore out, cursing everyone around her. She was hated in the maternity ward and Babs could never understand why people didn't speak to her during the periods when she was in control.

In early 1972, Babs began experiencing all kinds of neurological problems. She had headaches, problems with blurred and double vision, white flashes during her period, and other difficulties. She also began hearing voices. During this time, her daughter began having seizures and was diagnosed as brain-damaged. Babs took all types of pills to cope, and she eventually overdosed, ending up in the hospital for treatment.

It was during this hospital stay that I met Babs, so Tammy wound up Babs's history by listing eight problem areas that I, the psychiatrist, had to help Babs handle. First, her brain-damaged daughter; second, her feelings toward religion; third, sex; fourth, her relationship with her father; fifth, the relationship between her mother and father, including her mother's mental condition; sixth, her general family history; seventh, her problem of perceiving well-meant criticism as hostility; and eighth, her weight.

It is hard to say just when I came to trust the comments of

the ISH so implicitly. As I worked with each patient, I found that when I checked statements made by the ISH, they were always accurate. I was also able to cross-check information through hypnosis; once in a trance, patients would relive the same experiences and traumas mentioned by the ISH. For these reasons, I came to accept the information and help given by the ISH.

Tammy went on to explain that Babs had accepted the reality of having several personalities inside her. However, the idea also terrified her and I needed to be aware of this fear. It had prevented her from discussing her illness openly with me in the past, and I would have to cope with that unexpressed fear in the future.

To say that I was shocked by all this is an understatement. A psychiatrist is not trained to accept a built-in therapist within the mind of a troubled patient, yet that is what I had encountered. The logical, intellectual, unemotional ISH named Tammy had laid out Babs's entire life history, pinpointing the moments of stress that I would have to help her cope with in a better way.

My background had not prepared me to believe that such a situation was possible. I forced myself to analyze what I had seen and heard, and kept returning to the same conclusions. I had broken new ground in therapy, or at the very least, entered a field that no one else had written about. I was finally at a point where I could genuinely help all my patients, partly because of this little-known aspect of the patient's mind.

What I failed to realize at the time was the fact that the person controlling the body might not be the original personality. I have since learned that a dominant personality can control the body for thirty or forty years, despite the fact that such a personality may not be the original personality. If early problems are too overwhelming, the original personality will retreat into the mind, sometimes permanently, if treatment isn't given.

Babs began to lose her fear of her illness as we worked together to face the various crisis points in her life. Once we were able to introduce an alternative method for coping, there was little need for a personality split.

For example, through hypnosis I regressed Babs to age six to tackle the problem of Aunt Carmen. Babs knew that her aunt's behavior was wrong and she hated her aunt for making her do it. But Aunt Carmen had paid Babs twenty-five cents each time she participated in their sexual games. The ambivalence of her hatred of Carmen and her greed for the money had to be resolved.

I asked Babs to visualize Aunt Carmen in a chair in front of her, with the money she'd received in a bowl in her, Babs's, hands. I told her that it was necessary to give the money back to her aunt. When she finally realized that she had to give up the money she threw the bowl into the chair. Only then was she able to express and resolve her conflicting emotions about the incident.

Every episode like this had to be worked through to a proper conclusion, to eliminate the alter personality's hold on Babs's mind and to provide a way of expressing and neutralizing negative feelings. No episode could be ignored or further therapy would be stalled until it was resolved.

By May, Babs and Alice fused together to create a single, loving individual capable of having normal married sex and raising children. Babs completed the fusion after she saw her husband kneeling by the bed, praying that he would have only one wife. Babs finally realized that her husband truly loved her and she no longer needed Alice to fill in.

Babs was also learning to eliminate Lenore. When something upset her she would speak up, rather than letting anger build until Lenore burst forth as a personality.

Everything seemed to be going well. I was following the plan laid out by the ISH, a situation I still find surprising although I have long since stopped questioning it. We were going back to times of great stress through the use of traditional hypnosis, then coping with the problems that had resulted in a split.

By this time, I felt that I had developed an extremely open attitude toward new ideas and developments in multiple personality. However, none of my previous experiences prepared me for the next series of events in Babs's case. I received a frantic telephone call one night just before bedtime. "Dr.

Allison," Babs said, "I just can't stand this anymore. I don't want to go on like this. I'm not going to go on like this!"

I tried to calm Babs so I could understand what she was talking about. Finally she explained that she had gone to church, where she blacked out and apparently insulted her best friend. She said, "I was in church and I was having a good time with everybody. We were getting along fine, then something happened. The next thing I knew, my best friend told me I just cussed her out. My best friend! She's been standing by me through all this illness, the hospitalizations, and all the trouble. She baby-sits for me and is my best friend! I simply won't have her hurt anymore! I've just got to get rid of whatever it was that did this. I know it isn't me but it's in there and it's causing trouble and I'm not going to have it. Now what do I do?"

I had had Babs in therapy for many weeks at this point, and I had used every approach that I knew. She seemed to be progressing nicely, reducing the number of personalities and developing new ways to respond to stress. I had assumed she would continue in the same way until she was cured. Now she wanted an instant cure, and I didn't know what to tell her. She had been the beneficiary of everything I knew. There wasn't anything more to say, yet if I told her that, she would lose all faith in me and might revert back to her original condition.

As my mind raced over the possible options, I remembered how helpful Tammy had been. I decided that if the ISH could help the doctor, it could also help the patient.

"Okay, Babs, here is what you are to do," I began. Although I was very unsure of what I was saying, I spoke very positively. It was all a bluff, of course, but if Babs had faith in me and my guess about the inner workings of the mind was correct, there was a good chance my idea would work.

"Go into your bedroom," I continued, "lie down, and put yourself into a trance, as you have done in the office. Then go up into your head, up into your mind as far as you have to go to join with Tammy. And when you have joined with Tammy, I want you to ask her to bring God's healing power into you. Ask for that healing power and let whatever happens, happen. Don't try to make anything happen. Don't try to be specific about what you want to achieve. Just let God's healing power come down through you and do its work." I also told Babs to ask that all the good in her be fused together and all the bad cast out.

Babs took my advice. According to her husband, at eleven o'clock that night she knelt in prayer by her bed, calling on God to help her. As she kneeled, she suddenly began having a heated argument with Lenore. The intense anger in her voice was interspersed with softer words such as "yes, I do love Christ." Then she suddenly slid to the floor, smiled, and lost consciousness. He left her on the floor until she came to, approximately forty-five minutes later. When she regained consciousness, she pulled herself onto the bed and slept until morning.

When Babs awakened the next morning, I was frantically summoned to the house by her husband. I entered the most bizarre mental world I had yet encountered. This woman, mother of two children, wife, lover, and totally adult individual, had vanished. Her body was there, of course. Physically she hadn't changed; her weight, height, and general appearance were the same. But mentally she was no longer in her twenties. Babs was acting exactly like a five-year-old child.

There are many ways to take a life. When I was in training, my inability to act had resulted in the physical death of at least one patient. Carrie had also died, although her case involved a misreading of the danger signals. In Babs's case, I feared that although her physical body lived on, the Babs we knew was dead. As I approached Babs's bed, I couldn't help but feel that I had created another Carrie, although this time the woman would be a living, breathing monument to my inadequacies.

I had no idea what was happening to Babs, for she had entered a phase of development I had not previously encountered during the treatment of multiple-personality patients. I asked her where she was and she told me she was at home, waiting for Joan to come home from the hospital.

Joan hadn't been in the hospital for more than twenty years so I decided to test the range of her present-day perceptions. "And who is this man standing next to me?" I asked, gesturing toward Phil.

"That's Phil," she said, giggling shyly. "He's a nice friend."

All right, I thought, if Babs doesn't recognize her own husband, she's obviously experiencing life through a child's eyes. She probably doesn't know who I am either. "My name's Dr. Allison," I told her, speaking as one might to a nervous child. Whatever was happening, I silently prayed it was temporary. "I'm a friend too. I'll be talking with you some more later. Right now you should just rest and become familiar with everything."

I wasn't certain if Babs understood what I meant but she seemed perfectly happy as Phil and I left the room. I knew that she was perceiving life as a child again, and I realized that I would have to function as a child psychologist in the very near future.

"Phil," I said when we were out of hearing distance, "what seems to have happened is that we have uncovered the real Babs. Apparently, when her personalities fused, she returned to the emotional level of the child who first split apart years ago. She has an adult's vocabulary, yet her memory is impaired. I don't know how fast she will come out of this, but I know she is going to need your constant attention. You've got to take time off from your job until we see how she is progressing. Since she said she was waiting for her sister to come home from the hospital, she must be around five years of age at the moment and she will need to grow more before she can be left alone."

I sounded so knowledgeable, so sure of myself. . . . Phil seemed impressed at least. It made sense to him and had a logic that I could inwardly accept as well. However, I didn't have any time if I was right. It was a diagnosis I desperately wanted to believe, but I knew only time would tell if I was really fooling myself.

I visited Babs every day after that. On my second visit I found Babs sitting on the couch, fascinated by the television. The set was in color; the last television she could remember watching was a tiny black-and-white set that her parents had owned.

Babs greeted me as she would any friend. As we talked, I found that she still saw Phil as a "friend" and understood that the children were his. She remembered living with her grandparents in a small town to the south of her present home. In fact, she thought she was in her grandfather's house and was curious about the missing trees. Apparently there had been a number of trees she could look at through the front window.

Another day passed and Babs began to understand that the place where she was now living was her permanent home. She would not be going back to her parents. However, she still had no conscious memory of events occurring after her fifth birthday. Her memory was buried in her unconscious and the only way I could tap into it quickly and safely was to utilize Tammy. I told Babs that Tammy could help her remember all the years she had forgotten. I suggested that she ask Tammy to operate a movie projector in her head, showing her "films" of her life so that her entire existence would become a part of her conscious memory. She would finally know everything that had happened to her throughout her life, including the experiences of her alter personalities.

It is important to keep in mind that all of us have an Inner Self Helper whom we tap without realizing it. In the multiple-personality patient, the ISH is quite obviously separate. But when you have a choice to make and suddenly realize the right path, that "instinct" or source of knowledge is your ISH. You might call it your conscience. You certainly don't perceive it in a physical manner, as my patients do. Yet it is real and it is there. Thus, it was possible for me to work with the ISH even though I was convinced that Babs had fused.

Babs seemed to be showing psychic ability during this period. One day, for example, she was extremely hurt. She had been able to read Phil's mind and saw that he was lonely for Alice, the alter personality who had always made love to him. Even though Babs still had not come to understand Phil's role in her life, she was hurt by his longing for this other woman.

Theoretically, Babs could have been projecting her own concerns into her reaction to Phil. However, when confronted, Phil admitted that Alice had been on his mind. She was an aspect of Babs's personality who had given him physical pleasure. It was only natural that he would miss such experiences. Unfortunately, until Babs fully regained her memory, she couldn't understand that Alice was really part of herself, and that she and Phil could share what Alice had previously handled. All we could do was convince Babs that regardless of what Phil thought of Alice, he was pleased to have Babs around.

Babs viewed her children as playmates; she had no comprehension of their actual relationship to her. She noticed that her little girl, the one who was retarded, misbehaved frequently. Babs used to spoil the child, allowing her to act in ways that were wrong because she felt bad about the little girl's problem. But Babs as a five-year-old saw only another child being allowed to do naughty things that she, Babs, would get scolded for doing. No playmate was going to get away with that kind of nonsense while she had anything to say about it. She immediately began disciplining her daughter in a way she had never done before.

The results of this discipline were remarkable. The three-year-old little girl became toilet trained for the first time. "Five-year-old" Babs knew that three was too old for a child to be in diapers and plastic pants. She also disciplined her in other ways, making the child act in a manner fitting for her age.

Each day brought new changes in Babs's personality and development—she was literally growing up before our eyes. She came to understand her relationship with the two children and accepted them as her own. Then she comprehended the nature of Phil's relationship to her, although she did not jump back into the marital state. They underwent almost a repeat courtship, culminating in a new marriage ceremony. Babs wanted to be certain that she, the formerly hidden, main personality, made a marital commitment. After all *she* had never been involved with him, only her alter personalities.

With Babs fully adult, her complete memory returned. I took the time to reflect upon the case. I realized that in some ways I had blundered almost as badly as I had in Carrie's case. I had avoided responsibility by telling Babs to seek out a higher power when I had no idea what might happen. It was just the most convenient way to handle the matter over the telephone since I had no intention of rousing myself to go over to see her. I realized that I had been playing a very dangerous game.

Too many things might have gone wrong. Phil wasn't a trained therapist. The only reason he could help Babs was because he was not an emotional individual. His life was calm, orderly, and reasoned. He was able to accept his wife at each new stage, giving her an understanding of the world around her and helping her grow at whatever pace was necessary for her. Had he panicked or broken down, she could have had severe difficulties.

The entire situation was a miracle; there was no other way to describe it. The end result was truly awe inspiring. Babs became a whole adult person.

I vowed that in the future I would make certain such procedures were carried out in a controlled setting, preferably a hospital. Eventually I learned to utilize other doctors, psychologists, and nursing personnel as surrogate "parents" for patients emerging from fusion. I emphasized the difficulties they would have to face in dealing with someone who was physically an adult and emotionally a small child. It was important that my orders be followed without question since time was of the essence in taking a patient through fusion. We learned a great deal with every new case, and the risks decreased as I gained confidence and knowledge. I had begun my journey into the deeper recesses of the mind and I looked forward to further exploration.

Chapter 5

The Inner Self Helper and the Multiple Mind

Despite growing acceptance of multiple personality as a recognizable illness, many aspects, including the presence of the Inner Self Helper, remain mysterious. Although I believe there is a scientific basis for much of what we are learning, the reality of these aspects do not readily fit into the neat cubbyholes of accepted scientific thought. Patients' experiences are often at odds with the information in psychology textbooks, and many doctors would rather deny this reality than try to probe for its meaning.

As I met patient after patient suffering from the multiple-personality syndrome, I became increasingly aware of similarities in their perceptions and experiences. For example, let us consider the pattern of the Inner Self Helper. I have found that an Inner Self Helper has no date of origin as an alter personality does. The ISH is not "born" to handle a patient's unexpressed anger or violent trauma. It is present from birth and is present in a normal person as well as in a multiple, although in a multiple personality, the ISH appears as a separate individual.

Inner Self Helpers have no capacity for hate. They feel only love and express both awareness of and belief in God. They serve as a conduit for God's healing power and love. When they find themselves weaker than anticipated, they can call on a higher power to help.

The ISH never expresses a desire to lead a separate life.

Rather, the ISH wants to become one with the patient. The ISH also knows the patient's past history and can predict future actions with great accuracy.

The ISH has no conception of gender and refers to itself equally as male or female.

The ISH lacks emotions; it answers questions and communicates in the manner of a computer repeating programmed information. The ISH seems to be pure intellect and expects to be a working partner with the therapist.

As discussed previously, the ISH generally believes in reincarnation. There may be more than one ISH, each ranked in a hierarchy, and the highest ISH often speaks of being next to God. I have found it difficult to summon this type of ISH; it seems almost as though the therapist is not worthy of such contact.

Do I believe all this? I have no other explanation. These are concepts never before studied in depth and there is no way to judge what is happening other than by "gut" reaction. However, let me quote what some of the ISHs have said to me.

One ISH commented, "I am God." Another said, "I'm not God, you know, I can make mistakes, but I seldom do." Yet another wrote, "You ask what I am? Where do I live? I live in the minds and hearts of all men, for I am the creation of *God's* man-made knowledge of God. I am not mentally made. Yes, you could call me a teacher. Carla [the relevant main personality] now sees herself in relation to you differently; all that takes place around her is relative to the 'we' in her. We all are relative to every man's conscious mind, existing as teachers on the path of THE WAY. Not as preachers or those who teach the theory of God; we teach real inner truth.

"Our relativity is universal. As I can not be identified by a name or symbol which would hold any meaning for you, you can refer to me as Vida. But it is only a child [again we begin anew] to whom you will speak, an intuitive child at that. In any case, we will meet in time, for as we were, so shall we be again in eternity."

Once the patient taps into the ISH and starts using that source for guidance, the ISH becomes a teacher. Usually this happens after the patient has tried to work alone, ignoring this "conscience," and failed. Then he or she turns to the ISH out of frustration. As one patient commented concerning her relationship to the ISH:

> *I don't like being snuffed out and allowed to return by her directions. Oh sure, I sleep, eat and converse (like a dullard) and life (?) goes on, but where in God's name is the trail leading?*
>
> *Am I to be wrapped up and always protected in this way? I feel like a child who is allowed to go out and play (within very defined areas) but with a vigilant sentry always at the ready, complete with first aid kit and Band-Aids.*
>
> *I feel smothered and want to strike out at her. I know this is wrong, that she has my best interest at heart, but for crying out loud, do I have to remain subject to her idea of discipline? She has made it* clear *she's here to stay. How can I compete with her and hope to win? Am I meant to be second best? It is vexing to always be "odd man out."*
>
> *However, her enforced seclusion is really quite taxing. Nothing from nothing leaves nothing, as the saying goes.*
>
> *When she's here, she's here and that's that! She tells me only what she wants revealed and no more.*
>
> *And as to her methods—*
>
> *She can be quite a charmer, let me tell you. Sometimes I wonder who is the worst tormentor. Her or the others. She rubs my nose in old errors and is relentless in her revival of all my so-called foul deeds. Tight-fisted with her mercy. Small wonder I feel like an old hag!!*
>
> *I think I'm missing some part of this lesson she teaches, but I can't seem to grasp what it is.*
>
> *Perhaps you could influence her to lighten up a bit? She isn't perfect you know.*

I talked with the ISH of that particularly frustrated patient. She commented:

> *I have always been with her, regardless of what personality she assumes. I may be suppressed, but when called upon I can easily recall her past. I have been with her long before she stumbled on you. Call it fate, luck, or what-*

ever you choose, your paths crossed at a most crucial point in her life, when she and I were under an avalanche of evil.

In such situations my helpmates have been persons such as yourself. With all the past triumphs and failures relived, over and over, I have forced her to look at herself and admit her poor judgment. All my methods are not kind and she is in a most agonizing position now. I allow her mind to remain somewhat blurred and allow only limited communication between us. The lessons I teach are simple. Perhaps one day we will be able to discuss them. You see, I too, draw strength from entities like myself and as of late they have been few and far between. So at times like these, I retain the singular belief in a supreme creator of good and beauty, while in full awareness of the sometimes majestic powers of the Lord of Darkness. His powers are tremendous and once loosed, next to impossible to escape from.

Her perception of me is limited. I can keep her from being aware of my presence with no difficulty. However, she and the others can suppress my influence enough so my intellect does not affect her. Then the physical and negative emotions rule her.

Although I have been with her always, I have not been in control long enough to prevent this occurrence [*reappearance of a psychopathic personality*]. *I doubt she would ever have been able to come this far without your guidance and understanding. Only when tormented unmercifully did the* [*new alter personality*] *listen to me and then the* [*original personality*] *turned to you for help. Now she questions only my presence. I find this odd. You would think that she would, by now, admit my influence as quietly as she does yours.*

However, she does not, that will take time. And in the interim, your guidance remains essential to her. . . .

In time she will come to understand all the entities within her. You held the key which unlocked her mind and her own relativity. While I can and do hold possession of her now, it was not possible until the lock slid away from her mind, and then I too could finally be aided, enabling me to take charge of her in her despair.

As you know, I am neither ingenuous nor infallible but an integral part of her. And I am busily occupied just "keeping the lid on" and maintaining her health and welfare.

Once I accepted the reality of multiple personality and the concept of the ISH, I became curious about what was happening inside the head when any particular personality was dominating. I began questioning my multiple-personality patients and received a variety of answers, including: "Doctor, you know there is an infinite physical world outside this body. Inside the mind there is another equally infinite world in which I live. Each of us in there perceives that world differently."

One of my patients had more than thirty-five personalities. She imagined that each of these personalities had her own room within a boarding house inside her head. Each room was decorated in a manner appropriate to the occupant's personality. Linda, the angry one, had a room decorated in vivid red. Ann, the housekeeper, had brooms, mops, and vacuum cleaners scattered about her room. Although each personality retreated to her room to meditate and be alone, there was also a living room where they could get together to talk about matters of mutual concern. There was even a dungeon where someone could be placed if she was bad. In the dungeon, bread and water were slipped under the door. Only the ISH lived totally separately from the others.

One patient, Joy, described six personalities, including their physical appearances. She also told of conferences they held and re-created a script from one of them. The six, as seen by Joy, were:

LAURA: *She appears to be very tense and restless. She smokes one cigarette after another and watches the smoke as she exhales. Her hair is shoulder length and straight. She wears no make-up at all. She is wearing faded blue denim Levis and a green sweat shirt. She wears black cowboy boots. She wears several rings on each hand, but no other jewelry. She wears no nail polish, and her nails are ragged and short from biting. She never smiles and has a hard look about her.*

LINDA: *She appears to be very bored and uncomfortable. She is constantly looking about the room as if planning something. She occasionally smiles, but shows no genuine feeling. She lights up a cigarette and watches the smoke as she exhales as if hypnotized by it. She is wearing a tight-fitting black knit dress with a plunging neckline. It is extremely short, and she wears matching black nylons and shoes. She wears a large dinner ring on the index finger of her right hand, and large gold hoops in her ears. Her hair is bleached white-blond and worn in a bouffant gypsy style. Her make-up gives her a "Cleopatra" look which one cannot help but notice. She wears red nail polish. Her voice is low and soft. She watches people's reactions to whatever she says.*

MARY: *She appears to be very tense and worried. She does not smile and she looks extremely worn out and tired. Her eyes are dull. She wears a brown and white pants suit which looks very nice on her. She wears pearl earrings and a set of wedding rings. Her nails are well manicured and polished in a shade of deep pink. Her make-up gives her an innocent look. She wears her light blond hair in a long shag. She plays with her wedding rings as if she is very nervous and apprehensive. She is thin in build and her face appears drawn.*

FERN: *She sits very properly and looks demure and vulnerable. She appears uncomfortable and terribly shy. She does not smoke. She wears a knee-length suit of blue-green and yellow tweed. She wears no jewelry. Her hair is straight and blunt-cut to the chin. She wears no nail polish. She does not look at anyone directly.*

GALE: *She appears very confident and composed. She smiles frequently and has a sparkle in her eye. She does not look worried about anything. She occasionally smokes, but not to excess. She wears a blue sweater dress and a long necklace of blue and white beads with earrings to match. She wears red nail polish. She wears a pearl ring on her left hand and a blue dinner ring on her right hand. Her hair is shoulder length and falls loosely about her shoulders. The color is a golden blonde. She wears a moderate amount of make-up. She looks directly at others and listens carefully to what they have to say.*

JANE: *She appears to be rigid and overly composed. She smokes intently. She appears to be in deep thought. She only smiles occasionally. She is wearing a black-and-red pants suit, with black boots. She wears no rings, but does wear gold earrings and a necklace. Her hair is pulled away from her face. She wears very little make-up. She looks rather conservative. She is easily irritated by others and has very little patience. In spite of this she appears to have great understanding when confronted with a problem or situation.*

Joy went on to describe the conversation among the personalities at one particular meeting. I do not know whether this actually took place or was the creation of Joy's mind. I am sure that I have met the various personalities described and that the language and attitudes expressed in this conversation are typical of them.

GALE: *I think everyone should have, and needs, some kind of family.*

LINDA: *Speak for yourself. I have more fun without a family and I'm happy, so that means you're wrong.*

GALE: *I know damn well you're not really happy. You can't even be honest with yourself, much less anybody else.*

LINDA: *Why don't you mind your own business?*

JANE: *If we are going to discuss adult matters, why don't we show some respect for each other's feelings?*

LAURA: *Fuck a bunch of respect!*

FERN: *Do you have to talk like that?*

LAURA: *Why don't you go back in your shell where you belong? I was here before you were, anyway.*

LINDA: *And you're the most miserable of us all. At least I get along with men and that's more than I can say for you.*

LAURA: *So you like to fuck—big deal! You chase men like a bitch in heat.*

LINDA: *Nobody can stand to be around you, you and*

your four-letter vocabulary, and you've never been to bed with a man in your life.

JANE: *And you've never had an orgasm in your life. All you can do is fake it.*

LINDA: *You should talk.*

JANE: *At least I don't lie. Your whole life is a lie and I'm sick of hearing your bullshit. Mary is the only one of us that enjoys sex and can be satisfied by a man.*

MARY: *So I have orgasms. That doesn't get me love or happiness. And then all of you have to come into my life to make me more miserable.*

JANE: *You have made a lot of your own problems by repeating the same mistakes over and over again.*

FERN: *I think you are all too hard on her. She didn't have much of a chance to begin with, especially with Laura around.*

LAURA: *My life was fine until the rest of you bitches had to butt in.*

LINDA: *Now isn't that just too bad for you.*

GALE: *If it weren't for me, we would probably all be dead by now. I'm the most well adjusted of us all.*

MARY: *That may be so, but you lack any depth of character. Your sickeningly sweet smile is enough to make anyone sick after a while.*

GALE: *Dr. Allison likes me the best.*

MARY: *He doesn't know you that well. He knows me better than all of you put together.*

LINDA: *If we have to talk, why don't we talk about something interesting?*

MARY: *What's the matter? You get shot down by Dr. Allison?*

LINDA: *I don't need him. He's not the only man in this world. You are all too damn serious.*

GALE: *Running wild is your idea of fun, and what do you have to show for it?*

LINDA: *Look at all your conventional marriages. Husbands and wives are all screwing around on each other. Getting married is for the birds.*

MARY: *I happen to like marriage.*

LINDA: *Your marriage is exactly what I'm talking about. Neither of you are or ever were happy.*

GALE: *And you think jumping from one bed to another makes you happy.*

LINDA: *It's better than getting hurt. Life is a game and you have to use all the tricks in the book if you're going to get ahead.*

FERN: *This world would be a better place without people like you.*

JANE: *I sense a lot of bitterness in here.*

LAURA: *You're damn right I'm bitter. Why shouldn't I be? It's a cruel world and you have to be tough to survive.*

GALE: *There's a difference between being tough and being strong.*

MARY: *If I had been stronger, none of you would be here.*

LINDA: *That's past history.*

LAURA: *I need a drink.*

GALE: *You always need a drink.*

LAURA: *Son of a bitch! Why don't you all go to hell? It's none of your goddamned business what I do.*

MARY: *Why don't you just let her drink herself to death?*

LINDA: *Drinking is to be enjoyed. All you two know how to do is down drinks like a truck driver on Saturday night. I drink to have fun and be sociable.*

MARY: *You drink to have something to do with your hands until you can find a cock to go down on.*

LAURA: *That's telling her.*

GALE: *This isn't getting anybody anywhere.*

LAURA: *Shit! Linda would screw a snake if someone would hold its head!*

LINDA: *You're wasting your time if you think you're going to make me mad.*

GALE: *If everyone were like you two, it would be a hell of a world to live in.*

LINDA: *So who said life was a bed of roses?*

GALE: *That doesn't mean people can't be happy. If I had my way I would find a nice mature man to settle down with, and with luck, we would have children, live in a nice neighborhood, and be financially successful. People do still get married, you know, and some are even happily married.*

MARY: *You never were very realistic. I have nothing against marriage but it's not easy. Especially when you get married as young as I did. Reality hits you hard and fast. I admit I'm a dependent and insecure person. I need a man to take care of me. I admit that. But I thank God I never had children. I could never have taken care of them. I had a hard enough time taking care of myself, and I'm afraid, after my experience with my husband and other men, I could never trust any man to be faithful. One thing marriage has done is make me lose faith in myself as well as all others.*

LINDA: *Marriage may be fine for some people but not me. I have never found a man yet that won't play around if given the chance, and here the stupid wives are sitting home taking care of the kids while their husbands are out on the make. So why get married just to sit at home? Why not be out there having the same fun as the men are?*

LAURA: *So who needs men anyhow? Or anyone for that matter? You're better off making it on your own. Men are a pain in the ass. You can't depend on anyone but yourself. You're a goddamned jerk if you think you can trust anyone in this fucked up world. I know I may lead a lonely life but I don't get hurt, and that's what it's all about.*

FERN: *I feel like I have missed out on so much of life. There is so much to be experienced and enjoyed. And I have limited myself by being such a prude. I would have liked to meet someone who would have brought me out more. I have led a lonely life but not out of choice. At least I have learned from my mistakes.*

JANE: *The trouble with most people who get married is that they act on emotions rather than logic and common sense. Many have nothing in common but physical attraction. At its best, marriage is a compromise. If a marriage is successful, it's more the exception than the rule.*

The script that was written for me was confirmed by the others. It made me realize that a patient's alter personalities can be aware of one another's presence, as well as capable of "sitting down" and talking together within the mind. These conversations are carried out without the awareness of the main personality, however.

I don't know if such internal conversations can be developed into a therapeutic tool. The consistency of my findings indicates that perhaps it can, but this is for the future. Tragically, the patient who produced this particular script eventually committed suicide. However, the information I obtained from her in what proved to be a rather blundering manner enabled me to save other patients who might also have died.

Another unusual incident occurred when I talked to Renatta, an Inner Self Personality. She described what it was like to travel inside the mind. Renatta was one of more than thirty-five personalities eventually displayed by a patient who is now fused and leading a normal existence. Renatta wrote:

> *The places I visited will give you some idea of what happens when I am on the inside. I will describe each place in detail so you won't have to ask a lot of needless questions.*
>
> *The first place I went to is just behind the opening. You might call it a sort of "waiting room." All the different personalities "wait" to go back or come out. For me this happens quickly, but the others say it takes a few seconds to go either way.*
>
> *When someone is anxious or pushes to come out, there is a pressure type of pain that starts at the top of the forehead and travels down into the eyes. This sensation is somewhat like a light sensitivity during a migraine headache. No matter who is in control, if one of us is fighting to get out, the one who is out will feel the pain. As far as switching is concerned, that can take place in an instant if there is someone waiting.*
>
> *The colors that are there are somewhat muted and blend together like splotches on a wall. Some of them are large and some are small.*

When any of us travel higher into our head, the colors become lighter and more pure. For myself, this is a place of meditation. Anyone who goes there has a feeling of safety and security. When someone returns from there, he or she feels very euphoric and "high." This is where "heaven" is. The colors are mainly blue and yellow, with a little red. This is also where the others above Charity [the ISH] exist.

In the back of our head, the colors are dark orange, blending into brown and black. There are huge shapes of things suspended in midair. They look like large, sharp, jagged rocks. If someone wanted to hide, that would be the place to do it. When I go there, I feel very creepy, as if things were staring at me that I really can't see. I feel very cramped and stuffy there.

The place where most of us seem to stay is bright and clear. The colors surrounding it are soft, light shades of green, red, brown, and gold, all merging and drifting around us. This space is quite large, with more than enough room for us all.

We all have our own personal "hell" and Sylvia [the patient] is no exception. This is what I see when I travel into the depths of her mind. It is a place where bad thoughts, memories, things that have happened, and repressed feelings like hate and anger, are hidden, manifested, and grow into hideous monsters. They are black and very large. Most of the time they are motionless until they are stirred up by some kind of energy. Touching them brings pain. When I was there, my body felt very heavy, and I felt like I was covered with thistles and stickers. If you have too much contact with them, you can easily become one of them. That was the first time I was there and I never want to return.

When I look at the others, I see them in two different ways. The first is a mental picture of their physical features. They have different faces with arms, legs, hair, etc., even different voices. The second is really metaphysical. They appear as spheres, or balls of energy. Each sphere has a different color and brightness according to who and what they are.

The one you know as Charity, and the others like her, are different also. They too have physical bodies, but on the inside they are more like very dense clouds, bright and very active, hovering over us, but apart from the rest of us. We have more or less free rein. They guide us and tell us what needs to be done. They know everything; the rest of us, the "personalities," are limited in what we know.

Where there is communication between us, we can communicate through great distances or merge together and "talk." Two or more of us can merge and communicate that way or we can (and mostly do) send waves of feeling back and forth. If we wish to have a private meeting, we merge and place a shield around ourselves to prevent interruptions. In this way, we can work as one single entity for ourselves or as a whole for the body. Please remember we can also speak verbally. Our knowledge and information come from several different sources, one being Charity and those like her. Charity tells us what we need to know and gives us most of what we ask for. When Charity refuses, we can usually learn from Sylvia or other people. Information we are not supposed to have is easily erased from our minds by one of the higher ups. This happens to Sylvia as well when it is necessary.

As far as time is concerned, there is none. An hour on the outside is only a few seconds for us on the inside. The reverse is also true. This is probably why time is confusing, not only for Sylvia, but for all of us. We often get dates and events mixed up.

The way we move is also unusual. Depending upon our energy flow and the energy surrounding us, we can move from one place to another with great ease or great difficulty. If someone on the outside is using a lot of energy and under a lot of stress, it would be like trying to swim up a waterfall. At other times, under less stressful conditions, it is much easier. My feeling of floating and moving could be compared to the sensation of being under water when tides and currents push you about. We all drift quite frequently if we have nothing to hold onto, such as feelings or emotions.

Thus ends my paper for you and, I hope, your questions for me about what goes on inside Sylvia's head. While reading this, I hope you have kept in mind that we are as separate from each other as you and Sylvia are.

It is possible, I'm sure, for you to ask twenty patients the same questions, and receive twenty different answers. Any person has the potential to do anything he or she wishes to do and we are no exception, as I have proved by writing this to you. I was not allowed to write any more than I have. Some things are very private. So before I close, please remember my poem. I think it speaks for itself:

Caught on a breeze
I'm uplifted, extended
Way beyond the powers of the mind
I tell you what I see
How I feel
Only I know
And only you can imagine
Please remember that, Dr. Allison.
Signed, Renatta.

Within the framework of psychosynthesis, Renatta's descriptions fit the model of the mind. The region of hell would be the lower unconscious, heaven would be the upper unconscious, and the world of today would be the middle unconscious.

Is all this accurate? I don't know. It doesn't match standard, accepted scientific teachings, but neither does multiple personality in general. All I can do is probe, question, and record the answers I am given. Whenever a series of answers is consistent from patient to patient, I assume the information is probably accurate. However, it may be many more years before anyone truly understands the incredible complexity of the human mind.

Chapter 6

The Endless Depths of the Mind

Carrie's death shocked me into realizing just what kind of internal struggle took place within multiple-personality patients. As I observed each new case, I realized that the "evil" aggressor personality created to handle rage was capable of extreme violence. It appeared that, given enough time in control of the body, the aggressor personality would commit either murder or suicide. My first objective, therefore, was to help the patient reach a point where the aggressor was no longer needed.

As we have seen, the initial splitting usually occurs when the patient is overwhelmed by circumstances beyond his or her control. It happens at an early age, and the creation of alter personalities seems to be the patient's only escape route. However, in treatment, when the patient is shown an alternative way to view the early problems, the need for alter personalities is eliminated. The patient finds that expressing normal emotions is both possible and preferable. A woman tells her husband that she is upset when he comes home late for dinner, instead of letting her rage build up inside. She learns how to relax and enjoy normal recreation rather than hiding from the world until another personality takes over and seeks the night life.

As patients learn to cope, the various personalities fuse into one. It is difficult to describe this fusion scientifically because the exact mechanism is not yet understood.

There are three types of fusion—positive, negative, and incomplete—and three stages in a successful fusion. In positive fusion, all the positive personalities fuse and all the negative personalities are eliminated. In negative fusion, the opposite process occurs. Incomplete fusion means that the patient retains one or more alter personalities to maintain his or her social and/or psychological equilibrium.

For example, one multiple-personality patient had a sexy, hostile alter personality who was created at fourteen years of age when the woman was seduced by a priest. Her trauma was intensified because the priest had long filled the role of father figure, confidant, and friend. His intense sexual feelings for her added to the shock of the situation.

The alter personality had been formed as a defense mechanism. The woman created a personality who became a harsh seducer of men, an "individual" who controlled men by using sex as a weapon against them.

Eventually the woman came to me for treatment. During the early stages of treatment she learned that the priest who had seduced her had died. Suddenly there was no reason for the sexy, hostile alter personality to exist because the priest had triggered her creation and he no longer was alive. That personality simply disappeared. This is an example of incomplete fusion.

Incomplete fusion can also occur when the patient's environment is unstable. If a patient is having marital difficulties, problems with his or her family, a pressured job situation, or some other emotionally trying experience, he or she cannot sustain the effort necessary for a cure. It is very difficult to face one's self through therapy, and few individuals can handle both therapy and emotional turmoil at home. They manage to maintain control, living with incomplete fusion until they can create stability in their personal lives and effectively continue therapy.

Positive fusion is always my goal, and this requires the elimination of the negative, evil personalities. Such elimination can conceivably take years, although many of my patients have been helped in less than two years, and one woman was fused in a week. After fusion, only the original personality and the ISH remain. These two combine at a later period for the final fusion, after which further splitting is impossible. However, the resulting final fusion creates a totally new person in many ways. Such a person has to adjust to life all over again.

Most of my fused patients change their family situation. Divorce or long-term separation is common. Some change their names, others change their jobs. They feel as though they are new people and are anxious to understand feelings and concepts most of us have taken for granted for many years. It is more a new birth than a rebirth, for they *are* new individuals.

My curiosity about the "internal" mental process of fusion was, and is, strong. Nothing in the psychiatric literature I had uncovered to date provided any clues. The patient's appearance did not change in a drastic manner, yet it was obvious that something very special was going on inside his or her head, as evidenced by Babs's experience.

As my patients fused, I began to question them about the experience. I made tape recordings of the fusion period when I was present and, in at least one case, the boyfriend of one of my patients recorded the incident. I also had the hospital staff members make careful observations when the fusion occurred during a patient's stay on the psychiatric ward of the area hospitals.

There seems to be evidence that the patient frequently knows when fusion is coming. This is especially true when the main personality controlling the adult body is not the original personality. This was the situation with Babs, who had created what amounted to a second Babs to run the body when the original personality went under at approximately five years of age. The same was true for one of my male patients, Henry Hawksworth, who went under shortly after his third birthday. And it was also true for Yolanda, who came to the realization that she would shortly disappear while someone new, the original personality, took control.

Yolanda's background was fairly typical of my female patients'. She had been unwanted by a mother who tried to abort her and a father who eventually abandoned the family. She had endured a gang rape in her youth, and her personalities included both a drug addict–pusher and a religious zealot.

She was in her mid-twenties when I treated her. She approached fusion with mixed feelings. She accepted the necessity of fusion, for she knew that only when it occurred would she be mentally sound. However, she also realized that her fusion would be her "death" since she would no longer function on her own. She took a tape recorder to her room, sat down, and began talking. She was home at the time and felt the need to explain what she was experiencing. She said, in part:

> *Dr. Allison, this is Yolanda. It's now four-thirty in the morning, July sixteenth, 1976, and I'm going through a change. I may never be the same again. When you hear this, I will not be the same. I will be fused by then. There is so much I want to tell you but I can't. . . .*
>
> *I have felt a lot of pain, a lot of lopsidedness on the left side. The time has come for me to go. I do not go with sorrow or sadness. I go with some fear . . . fear of the unknown. But I am willing to do this. I am willing to cut off my right arm if that is what it takes to be "one." I am excited inside. I thank you for all that you have done for me. You have brought me to this point. I'm sorry that you cannot be here to see this. It's a feeling that words cannot explain. I hope that you can understand my feelings now.*
>
> *Right now I am experiencing a little discomfort in my brain. I'm with Oona* [Yolanda's best friend]*. I have been with her for five days. July nineteenth . . . It's a day that God has given me. I shall never forget this day . . . July nineteenth . . . I will become a whole person. . . . One person. . . .*
>
> *I have been waiting for this. Your pep talks brought me to this point, even though you didn't understand what I was going through. You accused me of many things that weren't true. I worked hard for this day to come and I love you for it. I feel no anger toward you.*

Yolanda was referring to conflicts she experienced in therapy. She would not have full memory of the actions of her alter personalities until after fusion. She had not fully accepted all the actions of her alters, although she understood who they were, how they behaved in general, and how she could free herself.

"It will all be over by Monday. I will stay in the hospital two or three days to recuperate, or however long it will take for me to learn to be one person . . . to function as one person. I have been with my dear friend, Oona, who has helped me through all of this. We've taped these problems that I have had."

Yolanda went on to discuss some of the friends she had made during her treatment, including one nurse who had been especially kind. She said she had visited her within the last couple of days, seeking support and saying good-bye.

> *I am willing to sacrifice anything that I have to [to become well], even my child, if that's what it comes to. Multiples must be able to accept the fact that they must give up everything to become one and I have done this. I have given up everything. I have been true and honest about what I've promised you about drinking. [Yolanda drank heavily and took all kinds of drugs. Actually only one personality was involved with this abuse, but the effects naturally caused problems for "everybody" sharing the body.] I have been honest about other things that I have promised you.*
>
> *I cut down on my pot smoking and it is not a necessity anymore. It was very hard for me to do. But I gave it up, and though it may not seem like much to you, I am very proud to have done this. I have cut down to the point of having no more than one joint a day. I have done this for myself, not just for you.*

Yolanda sounded very tired and she began to ramble. She was extremely weak and sounded very much like a person on her deathbed. In a few hours she would be but a memory, although her body would continue as strong and healthy as ever.

"I've grown up in many ways," Yolanda continued. "I'm not six. I'm not seven. I'm not eight or nine or ten. I'm all those ages.

"I want you to know that I love you, Dr. Allison, and I thank you for all that you have done. Someday God will bless you in many ways. Good-bye, Dr. Allison. Good-bye forever."

I thought the tape was over when Yolanda said good-bye, but her voice returned in a few moments.

"Dr. Allison, there is so much I have to tell you before I go," Yolanda continued.

> *I'm not sure how to put it. I have thought that some of your judgments about things were wrong at times. But I am willing to accept your theories and beliefs to make me better.*
>
> *This past week has been hell for me. I have experienced a lot of pain in my left side of my head, a lot of lopsidedness. It has been very painful.*
>
> *. . . The important point for me is that I am willing and able and want to become one. That is the most important part of being a multiple. To become "one" person you must be willing to sacrifice anything and everything, even your life, to become one person, even if it is only for one day.*
>
> *I've come to that point where I want to become one person. I want to be whole. I have had a lot of support from my friends and they are very excited for me. I have had the greatest support from Oona. She has been more than a sister to me. She is someone I love dearly. Oona has qualities in her beyond belief and I love her for those things. And I love her for herself. You are a very special man to have her help.*
>
> *Maybe someday I will also be able to help you. I want to. I want to be able to help you and many other multiples that are lost in this world and have no one in the world to turn to. I want you to use me as your vessel for healing. I still want you to guide me and teach me. I want to learn. I will miss you as I am now but soon I will be one and I will be with you.*

Then, as Yolanda's voice faded out forever, she whispered: "Being multiple is hell, but the gift of becoming one is worth the lopsided pain. It's well worth it. . . . It is well worth it."

Yolanda's fusion apparently occurred quietly—an act of death and rebirth that passed in peace. If there was any sort of violent struggle, screaming, or hollering, it went unnoticed by her neighbors. But Yolanda's experience was not altogether typical of what I encountered. Others went through a violent internal struggle.

Carla went through a fusion approximately eight months before Yolanda. Her fusion was filled with drama, high adventure, and a struggle to the death, all taking place inside her head. Some of the "action" was described at the time. Other parts were remembered after she was whole again.

Carla envisioned a large battlefield with her main personality and her violent, evil alter personality dressed head to toe in armor, prepared to fight to the death. They wanted to tear out each other's throats but were held apart by the less violent but equally evil alter personality named Anna, and by the ISH, Zoie. This particular patient had revealed between thirty and fifty different alter personalities over the years and they were all lined up like spectators in her mind.

Although this massive number of alter personalities was unusual, it is a logical result of the illness for some patients. The technique of splitting originally occurs out of necessity, but some patients find it an easy way to get through life. A personality might be created to handle even a minor problem, then be discarded a few minutes or hours later, never to be seen again. For those few moments, a unique individual exists. In Carla's case, for example, an alter personality once took over to watch the rerun of a children's television program that Carla had wanted to see when she was growing up.

Carla was in the conference room of an area hospital, under the close supervision of the staff, when her fusion began. Suddenly she slumped to the floor, an action triggered by the violence about to start in her head. She began rolling around the floor, smashing her head against the linoleum, clawing at her face and arms, and generally behaving like someone engaged in a life-or-death struggle. "I'm going to kill you if it's the last thing I ever do!" she screamed, grabbing her own throat with such force that her fingers embedded themselves deeply in the skin. I grabbed her wrists and pulled them away, amazed at the strength with which she resisted me. The room had been cleared of furniture so that she would not be able to injure herself seriously as she thrashed about.

"No! You're not going to kill me!" a different voice shouted, both voices coming from Carla's lips. Even though I was prepared for the violence of her battle, it was a disconcerting sight to witness. The medical staff and I had to be constantly on the alert to be certain that she didn't actually injure herself.

The battle continued for what seemed like hours, but only thirty minutes actually passed before there was a tremendous heaving motion and Carla, her body covered with bruises, finally relaxed. Her eyes opened and a peaceful expression of joy appeared on her face. Carla was gone, having emerged victorious only to retreat into the mind to rest. Her Inner Self Helper, Zoie, was in control, making a final appearance. She stayed in charge of the body until the next day, when the original Carla was sufficiently rested to begin a new life as a whole individual.

Like Babs, Carla emerged with the memory and reasoning of a tiny child. It would be many days before she could function completely on her own.

Another violent episode occurred with Enid, a patient who experienced fusion in the presence of her boyfriend, Bill. He kept a tape recorder going throughout, although he became more physically involved than I had in Carla's case. He talked with the two personalities doing battle together and tried to cradle Enid's head when the evil side of her attempted to kill her by smashing her head into a hard wall.

Enid battled against Gretle, her violent alter personality. Once again there were outward signs of physical violence, although there were pauses during which Bill was able to talk with both individuals. Incredibly, Bill reported that Gretle would grab hold of him and try to drain some of his physical strength when she saw she was losing. It was as though she could sap his energy to increase her own reserves, much like a vampire sucking blood from its victim. He would have called me for assistance but he was too busy trying to handle Enid.

At one point Bill tried to convince Gretle to stop fighting.

Gretle had never admitted that she was an alter personality. She believed she was real, a fact which Bill disputed. "Enid fabricated you," he told her.

"She didn't give a fuck," Gretle said. "She was just copping out."

Gretle meant that the main personality was running from her problems when Gretle was created. Yet this recognition did not mean that she accepted the fact that she was a part of Enid's mind rather than a unique individual in her own right. Bill persisted, saying:

"She was copping out and she created you. SHE CREATED YOU! And now she doesn't need you anymore. She thanks you. She can't thank you enough for being here when she needed you. But you MUST GO!"

Once the fusion had taken place, Enid put her thoughts on paper: "This is a description of my own, of an extremely crucial battle in which I and another part of myself fought TO THE DEATH!" The emphasis was Enid's, and she related a battle which involved herself, the evil Gretle, and what she said were hundreds of inhuman, violent followers of that hateful side of herself.

Enid's main personality had submerged many years earlier and a second personality controlled the body most of the time following the initial split. The real Enid only began appearing toward the end of her therapy, which led to the successful fusion. As she explained:

> *My first appearance was mid-June, although I was unable to stay out long at first. I was informed that my presence made Gretle uneasy. Although she exercised more strength than I, she could not keep me in her total control. I came in and out as my adviser* [*her ISH*] *felt it necessary. I learned much in my absence and I learned rapidly what Gretle's trip was. I felt strong desires to regain control of myself and erase Gretle. I grew stronger and stronger until I was ready to face her—and life again. I really wanted it!*

Enid created her first alter personality at an older age than most of my other patients. I have discovered that it is extremely rare for anyone to develop multiple personalities for the first time once adolescence has begun. This may have to do with emotional growth or some change in body chemistry. I don't really know why, nor am I familiar with any research on the issue. Enid had split several times when young but did not completely recede into the mind until age thirteen.

Enid's father was extremely cruel and violent. He had wanted a son and he never stopped punishing Enid for being the "wrong" sex. He frequently beat both Enid and her mother. When she was thirteen, she faced yet another seemingly endless series of beatings and decided she could no longer take it. She went under, letting the suppressed anger she felt toward the man become personified in the form of Gretle. Gretle was strong enough to handle the father's violence, but as the years passed, she became almost as violent as the father whose actions resulted in her creation.

Enid told of fighting with Gretle for a number of days before the major confrontation. Then, on the day fusion took place, she said: "It began gradually with pain in all parts of my body, accompanied by hallucinations. I saw Bill in exaggerated situations with many different women. I knew Gretle was responsible, showing me things she knew would upset me. I decided that I could not allow any of these to pierce my heart, for I could not allow myself to feel emotional pain. I refused to be weakened in that way. Winning myself back was far too important to risk."

Enid went on to describe a violent battle. "Gretle continually tried to kill me in any way she could. When she was on the outside she was banging my head on walls, floors, dressers, beds. Bill tried to restrain her."

During a lull in the battle, Bill left the room for a moment. Enid wrote:

> *Without my knowledge, Bill left the room and found a crucifix Gretle had hidden. Returning, he held it in front of my face while Gretle was out, and I blocked all escape passageways. Finally he forced her to open her eyes. All I know is she screamed in agony and was no more.*
>
> DEAD.

Feeling more like a victor than a murderer, I felt more than proud of myself. My body was sore and bruised but I knew I would heal and be a normal person. It was the greatest feeling I've ever known!

The experiences related by fused multiple-personality patients do not in any way reflect established scientific thought about the mind. Does this mean that the people relating fusion experiences were actually relating the hallucinations of a sick mind? I don't know. I am only certain of their sincerity and what has been witnessed and recorded by others. The situations seem to be fairly consistent and the patients were fused when they were over.

The religious aspect may be real and it may result from the chance fact that most of my patients have strong religious beliefs. The ideas of heaven and hell are very real to them. They feel themselves torn between forces of good and evil during their illness. I am convinced that good and evil are very definite, very real forces. I view them as outside influences on the patients' lives. My patients who have related their experiences reinforce this by talking about the devil, Satan or some other specific evil entity fighting against God or His representatives.

Many of my fellow psychiatrists would view these concepts as superstitious nonsense. They want to deny everything that can't be proven conclusively by scientific methods. They may be right, but they also may be closing themselves off from a reality greater than we can comprehend with our present knowledge. After all, most of the advances in medical science that we take for granted would seem miraculous to people living only 150 years ago when barbers handled many of the medical procedures!

I have been careful to refrain from pushing my value system onto my patients, however. I consistently avoid suggesting the idea of a conflict between good and evil. I remain open to whatever value system they need to use in order to get well. This openness has, at times, enabled patients to speak more freely than if I were rigid in my thinking.

However, I could not contain myself from discussing my work at various psychiatric association meetings. I felt that others should be aware of my experiences in case they encountered similar problems. Naturally I played down some of the religious aspects, including the exorcisms, knowing the professional reaction would be harshly negative.

Surprisingly, the one person who was comfortable with the concept of exorcism was my father. I sent him a paper I had written on the subject, hoping to improve our relationship in any way possible. I thought that he might be interested in my work in a field that, in a sense, had been his own. He sent back the paper with some notes, primarily adding Scripture references that reinforced what I had written. He seemed to accept the entire concept. Unfortunately, my supposedly open-minded colleagues could not.

The main opposition came from the psychiatrist who had been head of the peer review committee. He was now head of a committee concerned with quality control and in a position to dispute my diagnosis and other aspects of my work. Once again he charged that I was doing "something" unethical, improper, and experimental. His charges were quite vague, however, as though I was an evil force that everyone could sense, so there was no need for further explanation.

His committee wrote a report to the hospital department of psychiatry recommending that my privileges be restricted so I could no longer admit known multiples to the hospital. To make matters worse, one of the peer review committee members didn't even bother attending the meeting where my work was discussed. He signed the document without the slightest firsthand knowledge of what was going on.

I was depressed by these actions. I wanted someone to attack specifically the treatment techniques I had evolved. I wanted to be able to lash out against specific charges. I felt outrage and deep hurt, and had no way of purging my emotions except to complain to family and close friends who, I suspect, got a little tired of my tirades.

When the peer review committee turned in its report to the hospital department of psychiatry, it recommended that my privileges be restricted in that hospital.

A meeting of the entire hospital department of psychiatry was set and I was uncertain what to do. I decided to go to church and pray for guidance, since I was so agitated that I could not handle the problem objectively. As I prayed, I kept thinking of the word "pride." At last I felt that I understood what was happening. In my zealousness to spread my findings and, in many instances, my cures, I had become quite boastful. I was presenting information in a way that was threatening to those around me, many of whom had treated my patients unsuccessfully before the patients came to me.

Admittedly, when I discussed my treatment plan with those who had used more traditional approaches and failed, I was setting, in effect, psychiatric standards. One of the psychiatrists who attended a meeting at which I spoke said, "If we don't follow your approach, are we then guilty of malpractice?" Of course, one could reach that conclusion if one wanted to stretch the definition of malpractice. After all, the other treatment approaches being used in my area did not seem to be working, and my methods did. Therefore, to use an approach that had not been shown effective was, in essence, malpractice.

My answer, at the time, was, "You said that, not I." It was not an approach that would win friends, and as I reflected on my attitude, I realized that much of the hostility I generated was my own doing. It was not so much what I said but the way I had said it.

When the entire department of psychiatry voted on the committee recommendation to restrict my privileges, they voted in my favor. Many of the members were professional friends who did not necessarily approve of my methods but who recognized my sincerity and my right to use them. Some felt that I had been rather boastful and perhaps arrogant in the way I handled myself with others and were upset about that. But they also realized that such human weakness did not represent malpractice or bad professional judgment as it related to the patients. That is why they voted so favorably.

To placate those members who were upset with the way I worked, I agreed to limit my admission of multiple-personality patients to genuine emergencies only. I knew they could not argue the need for that option, and the matter officially ended there.

Later I realized that it was important for me to withstand

the pressures of my colleagues. I also found that I had to be more tactful in my presentations to others or I would be in serious trouble. The fact that the trouble was unwarranted really didn't matter. My pride could be my downfall, hindering my ability to practice all that I had learned.

I tried to use a more tactful approach in dealing with the peer review committee members and others in the medical profession, and this seemed to help. I remained controversial, but I had diffused their attack. I still faced periodic criticism, but I continued my work.

Chapter 7

Discovering the Male Multiple Personality

The majority of cases recorded in this book have dealt with female multiple personalities. This is also true for psychiatric literature in general. If the number of reported female multiple personalities is small, the number of known male multiples is even smaller.

There was a time when I might have concluded that male multiple-personality patients were unlikely to exist because so few men suffer the same kinds of trauma endured by my female patients: rape or extreme sexual abuse. However, as first one and then another male sought my treatment, each showing signs of multiplicity, I realized there were no certainties in this field. If the trigger wasn't sexual abuse, it could still be trauma so severe that the child had to flee inside his head, creating a new personality to take his place.

In one case, the trigger for a male multiple personality was a three-year-old boy's inability to measure up to his emotionally disturbed father's standards. He was constantly abused by a man who was completely inconsistent in his demands. What was acceptable behavior for the child one day might not be proper the next even though the circumstances were the same. The small boy suffered continual physical and verbal abuse, culminating in a horrible incident in which his clothing caught on fire when he stood too close to a fireplace. This terror, coupled with a fear of how his father would react to his crying (unmanly in his father's eyes), led to the creation of his first alter personality. Although there was no sexual trauma, all the other factors common to multiples were present when the emotional trauma of the fire caused him to "split."

After I realized that sexual violence need not be a trigger, I discovered another reason for the apparent scarcity of male multiple personalities. Our society accepts, and often exalts, male violent behavior as a normal masculine trait; when women act similarly, however, they are often considered mentally ill. When one of my patients, Henry Hawksworth, was taken to court to answer criminal charges stemming from a brawl involving Johnny, his violent alter personality, the judge found the incident humorous. Johnny had single-handedly and successfully fought off a motorcycle gang and the police.

Henry was in charge of the body while in the courtroom and appeared to be gentle, intelligent, and refined, all traits he did indeed possess. The judge assumed the violent fight stemmed from too much booze and an attempt to emulate television programs. He laughed at Hawksworth and told him to stop drinking so much and avoid TV cowboy shows.

Even Hawksworth's wife, Anne, did not realize the type of help her husband needed. She felt that alcoholism was the only difficulty he faced. She encouraged him to participate in Alcoholics Anonymous, but the idea that he might be mentally ill was never given serious consideration.

Similar stories can be told about other men. Society finds an excuse for their irrational behavior. It might be drinking, or office pressure, or just a case of "feeling his oats."

Women, even in these days of women's liberation, are expected to behave in a more consistent manner. Erratic behavior is not tolerated. A man can tear up a bar and nobody takes it seriously. Let a woman engage in such violence, though, and she will probably be forced into psychiatric treatment by the court. Thus, her illness is more likely to be discovered. Male multiple personality, therefore, is probably not as rare as it seems; the conditions of our society simply make it a less common diagnosis.

My work with male multiple-personality cases has taken me

in some new directions. For example, previously I had been convinced that the Inner Self Helper, who is really the conscience, could somehow prevent an evil alter personality from committing the ultimate sin—murder. Accidental death is always possible, of course, but in all my earlier cases, the violent personality had always been controlled by a rescuer personality under the direction of the ISH. Fighting was common, but the rescuer would never allow deliberate murder, or so I thought.

However, the reality appears to be different, although I do not understand why. A current case of mine involves a man whose multiplicity has not been conclusively proven, although he exhibits all the characteristics of a multiple personality. Several psychiatrists have tested him in addition to myself, and he seems to be a classic Dr. Jekyll and Mr. Hyde, with one good and one bad personality. As "Mr. Hyde" he appears to have committed several deliberate murders. The good personality, who is fortunately in primary control of the body, had no knowledge of the crimes, which were totally against his personal moral code. However, no rescuer ever came forth to stop the deaths.

Although this case is not yet conclusive, I was involved with another man who is now on death row. His case is worth examining since he too committed deliberate murder despite the presence of his rescuer personality.

Mark Petroff was an odd-looking youth in his early twenties when he was first referred to me by the courts. He had jet-black hair that stuck straight out from his head, as though he were perpetually frightened.

He had been arrested for arson and there seemed no way he could beat the charge of having burned six homes. When he was caught in his car, his shoes had soil deposits from the homes. He also had various incendiary devices, matches, and other items identical to those used for the burnings. Although he accepted the idea that he was responsible for the arson, his only memory was of watching the last house when it was in flames. He didn't know how he happened to have the incendiary devices or when he might have driven to the sites of the houses.

Mark's lack of memory was the first clue to his illness, although I did not initially think of multiple personality in connection with his case. At the time I only knew he had tremendous emotional problems stemming from the death of his mother in an accident for which he felt responsible.

As I talked with Mark and studied the court records, I learned that he and his brothers had always had a grudge against society. Since well before their teen-age years, they had engaged in various crimes, including burglary and the buying, selling, and use of narcotics. Although their records showed conviction for only relatively minor infractions of the law, they had developed the expertise of professionals. Sadly, I was never able to work with Mark long enough to learn what first triggered this antisocial behavior, much less to alter it.

Mark's father worked for the Forest Service as a pilot. Whenever a forest fire broke out, his father would fly over the area, dumping chemicals to stop the flames. He was frequently away from home, leaving his wife to discipline the children.

Mark's mother was the mainstay of the family and a strict disciplinarian. She managed to contain her sons' criminal activities and may have had a hand in their relatively minor conviction record. Unfortunately, her influence came to an abrupt and tragic end.

One summer when Mark was in his early teens, his mother took the boys on vacation while their father was at work. They were traveling around the countryside in a van, and Mark was bored. He was impatient to get back to his girl friend, and his mother agreed to return home a day ahead of schedule.

The family was almost home when an irresponsible driver forced them out of their lane, sending the van careening toward the center divider, out of control. Seconds later the van crashed and Mark's mother was beheaded before his eyes. Her head was completely severed from her body, and the boys were also badly injured.

When the surviving brothers were taken to the hospital, Mark found that he had the least pain and the fewest broken bones. As he watched one of his younger brothers writhe in agony from the numerous breaks and bruises covering his body, Mark felt an almost overwhelming sense of responsibility. He relived the sight of his mother's head separating from her body as she was killed instantly. It was a nightmare that may have replayed itself endlessly inside his head, although he never shared his feelings with anyone else. In fact, all the boys were so calm after their initial emergency care that no one realized the trauma they had endured.

Psychiatrists are sometimes guilty of an incredible lack of common sense. Here were several brothers who had witnessed the horrible death of the person closest to them. They had been in a terrifying crash and had experienced events that were bound to create fear, anxiety, and, in Mark's case, guilt. They desperately needed counseling, possibly for an extended period of time, yet they received no such help.

The minister at the hospital talked with the boys, offering them spiritual guidance. He may have been comforting to a degree, but he could not and did not attempt to cope with their emotional problems. That was left to the head of the psychiatric department, who examined the boys very briefly.

The psychiatrist watched the boys playing in the hospital, racing their wheelchairs and engaging in other youthful pranks. Since they appeared to be happy on the surface, he saw no reason to probe their minds any further. All psychiatrists are trained to recognize that superficial indications of joy and sorrow may not reflect a patient's inner emotions. Common sense should have kept the examining psychiatrist from writing the boys off as "adjusted" so soon after the crash. Unfortunately, he avoided the responsibility of deeper probing, and the brothers were eventually released from the hospital.

Mark was filled with conflicting emotions. He felt overwhelmingly guilty for "causing" his mother's death and extremely angry with society in general. He went to live with his grandmother, who couldn't control him, and his father, who spent even more time away from home. Mark became even more violent and undisciplined, burning homes, committing burglaries, and generally engaging in criminal activities in the wealthy areas near his home.

The sad part about Mark is that he had so little contact with psychiatrists who could help him. My involvement was not as a therapist but as an evaluator for the court system.

My first meeting with Mark was inconclusive. He accepted the fact that he had set the fires, but had no memory of the incidents. I could tell that he needed more treatment, but Mark wouldn't allow it because of the other prisoners' attitude toward psychiatry.

I had no idea that Mark was a multiple personality when I first talked with him, but I was absolutely convinced that he was extremely sick. My report to the court indicated that he was not "insane" and could not be considered innocent for that reason. However, jailing him would be senseless. He needed intensive counseling, and if he had to be locked away, my recommendation was a mental ward where he could work out his emotional problems.

Mark discussed the case with the other prisoners in his cell area, and they ridiculed him about the possibility of hospital confinement. Mental hospitals were a cop-out, according to the other prisoners. They were for sissies who couldn't take jail. A real man would go to jail.

The prisoners' comments affected Mark deeply. Although he seemed to recognize the validity of my diagnosis, he could not allow any challenge to his manhood. He arranged to see another psychiatrist and put on an act. I don't know exactly what he said and did, but he accomplished what he'd wanted. The other psychiatrist reported that Mark was simply a rotten individual.

Mark was sent to the California Youth Authority for a year. During his confinement he was accused of stealing another boy's notebook, an action he vehemently denied. However, when a check of his locker was made, the notebook was found inside. Mark had no idea how it had gotten there and suspected he might have been framed. Actually, as I later discovered, an alter personality had stolen the notebook, and Mark really had no knowledge of the incident.

There were other hints concerning Mark's problems. At one legal hearing his father had testified that there seemed to be two distinctly different sides to Mark. One morning he might be a Bible-toting religious fanatic who wouldn't even step on an ant, fearing God's wrath for injuring the tiniest of creatures. By evening, however, Mark would embark on another destructive rampage.

While Mark was in jail, California's law was changed. It now seemed possible that Mark could sue the state for having operated an unsafe freeway. The accident that caused the death of Mark's mother could not have occurred had there been a proper median barrier. This negligence on the part of the state highway authority could become the basis for a lawsuit.

It had been three years since the accident, too long for a lawsuit to be filed unless it was ruled that Mark was mentally disturbed at the time of the accident and unable fully to understand what had happened. Actually this was a technicality. Emotionally disturbed or not, Mark didn't sue at the time because the law did not allow it then. It was only several years later that it even became possible.

Mark's father was the instigator of the lawsuit and the lawyer asked me to do another psychiatric evaluation of Mark. The youth still could not remember what went on during the burnings so I hypnotized him and asked to speak to whoever burned the houses. All of a sudden an enraged monster emerged. It was Mark's violent alter personality and the discovery shocked me. When I called him "Mark," he cursed me loudly and made it quite clear that his name was Carl.

I interviewed Carl as best I could. He couldn't decide whether to tell me to go to hell and refuse to say anything further, or to answer my questions in the most abusive manner possible. Fortunately, he chose the latter approach and I gradually learned his history. He had been "born" at the age of seven when a gang of teen-age boys had grabbed Mark and brutally raped him.

It was a classic case, triggered by a particularly brutal form of sexual abuse. The sexual connection convinced me that other alter personalities were involved and I immediately began to call them out.

One of the first personalities I discovered was a rescuer. Mark had become involved with smugglers who brought narcotics and other contraband into the United States by boat. Carl had signed on as a crew member after the original crew went to jail. When the ship was raided a second time, this rescuer took control, adopting a naïve, innocent attitude toward the whole matter. He convinced the police that he knew nothing about the true nature of the ship's cargo and was totally shocked to find himself involved in a criminal activity. His story proved so convincing that he never went to jail or was in any way linked to the smuggling ring.

I was extremely concerned by all this, and wanted to help Mark. However, I felt I could not act as his therapist, hearing all his deepest fears and secrets, and as an advisor to his attorney, since he was trying to manipulate the legal system. He had come to me for help with what he considered his most serious problem—being a Peeping Tom. Arson was fine; he didn't consider that nearly as serious as his voyeuristic tendencies.

While Mark was under treatment, I became indirectly responsible for beginning a chain of events that would have disastrous consequences for both Mark and another patient, Lila, who operated the biofeedback machine in my office. Because Lila had been so helpful in Babs's case and because she was progressing so well in her therapy, I introduced the two of them formally, hoping Lila could keep in touch with him for me. At the time it seemed like a good idea, since they had often met in the office and appeared to like one another. Mark had not yet given me any reason to believe he was as severely disturbed as he later proved to be, and Lila was much more stable than she had been when she began treatment. In retrospect, this course of action was a mistake, but at the time it seemed both logical and possibly beneficial to both, and there was no way I could have predicted the results.

What ultimately happened, however, only confirmed my belief that medicine is a practice, not a profession. My "brilliant" idea backfired horribly. Mark and Lila did become casual friends who enjoyed each other's company. However, Mark's psychopathic personality, Carl, became the lover of Lila's violent alter personality, Esther. The worst in each of them had found a common bond in their hatred of both the world and the main personalities of the bodies in which they were living.

During this period, Lila was living in a small apartment in the same building where Nancy, my secretary, lived. Nancy had helped her find the place so she could keep an eye on

Lila. Nancy and I were stunned when Carl decided to move in with Esther, a situation both Mark and Lila accepted.

Mark's parole officer was outraged with Mark's new living arrangement. He called me and the psychiatrist from the California Youth Authority to discuss what could be done. He was convinced that the two young people should either marry or separate. Living together was not at all acceptable.

I was actually rather pleased with the arrangement despite my personal views about cohabitation without the sanction of marriage. Lila had shown suicidal tendencies, and I was pleased that she was receiving full-time emotional support from someone who cared about her. Carl did not come out when Lila was around, so there was no risk to her safety in that regard. Since Mark himself was strongly supportive, this rather abnormal situation was beneficial for Lila.

Lila was also a good influence on Mark. She was able to keep him in line, and she gave him a sense of purpose. However, neither one was mentally or emotionally ready for a true marriage and there was little chance they would stay together after one or both of them returned to sound mental health. Under the circumstances, living together seemed to be an ideal temporary arrangement. Marriage, on the other hand, would have been a socially acceptable disaster.

I was overruled. A wedding was planned and I went along to the rehearsal. But even that event was doomed. Lila underwent a completely unexpected and startling transformation, and I was grateful I was on hand to prevent further disaster.

Until the wedding I had assumed that Lila, the main personality, was also the original personality. As I later learned in therapy, this was not the case. The original personality, Susan, had gone under at age three, so thoroughly traumatized that she hadn't made another appearance for fifteen years. Lila's progress in therapy finally made Susan's appearance possible—and the change occurred as she walked down the aisle during her wedding rehearsal!

She suddenly blanked out, then opened her eyes wide. She looked all around the room, her mouth agape, then looked down at her wedding dress and back up at the people around her. Her face contorted slightly and she started to cry. In a high-pitched, childlike voice, she said, "I don't want to get married. I don't like this. I don't want to get married." Tears came to her eyes and her nose began to run. She started to wipe it on the sleeve of her dress but someone had the presence of mind to give her some tissues. She blew her nose awkwardly, then cried some more.

Most of the observers had no idea what was going on and probably thought Lila had a case of last-minute nerves. Fortunately, none of them realized that Lila had been replaced by a three-year-old child.

Desperately, my mind raced over possible courses of action. Should I stop the wedding? On the one hand, I was suddenly faced with a new personality I'd never met. Surely that was an indication that Lila wasn't as stable as I'd previously thought. On the other hand, both Lila and Mark were of legal age under state law. Neither was legally insane, and both were therefore fully competent to make decisions on their own, at least as far as the courts were concerned. I would have to go through a lengthy process to prove there was reason to deny them the right to marry, and there was no time. They were both aware of one another's mental problems and had entered this agreement with their eyes open, although I questioned their judgment. I decided I could only stop the wedding if this new personality dominated the body and refused to return to that part of the mind from which she had come. Actually, if I had failed to put Lila back in control, Susan would have stopped the event anyway with her own childish actions.

Desperately, I reasoned with this new personality. I talked to her as I would any unruly child, finally working out a compromise. She agreed to return control to Lila on the condition that when the wedding cake was cut at the actual ceremony, she could have the first piece. Otherwise she would probably have yelled and screamed throughout the ceremony.

Susan retreated as promised and the rehearsal proceeded with no further trouble. During the actual ceremony the next day, Lila looked as radiantly normal as a bride could be. When she started to cut the cake, her hand paused and her eyes glazed over. Three-year-old Susan returned, awkwardly cutting a huge slice of cake, which she stuffed eagerly into her mouth, smearing her lips, nose, and cheeks with the white icing. When she was finished, she grinned happily while someone cleaned her face with a napkin. Then she retreated again, returning only when I called her back for treatment in my office.

The marriage itself was as strange as the wedding. Lila and Mark grew nervous around each other and were unhappy with the relationship. Esther and Carl, on the other hand, took great pleasure in one another. They engaged in all kinds of sexual adventures with each other and also shared a taste for unusual entertainment. For example, they would go down to the beach whenever there was a full moon, then run about screaming and howling as though they were possessed. This had nothing to do with their mental illness. It was simply their way of having fun and "freaking out" anyone who might chance to see or hear them.

As expected, the marriage didn't last. The attraction of the two psychopathic personalities was not strong enough to keep the couple together. They split from each other in a fairly short time. Mark moved in with another girl and became increasingly bitter about women in general.

Mark had always had trouble with his sex life. The trauma of the gang rape he'd experienced was intensified by his mother's attitude about sex. She felt sex was dirty and beat him severely for normal, youthful sexual exploration. The first time he kissed a girl, she caught him in the act and beat him for it. She never described sex as a natural and desirable act. Rather, she told him that sex could give a boy a fatal disease.

When Mark was sixteen, he had his first homosexual encounter. One or two homosexual encounters are not unusual in a boy's life during the early years of sexual awakening. The extreme guilt and fear Mark experienced were also quite normal for his age. However, Mark's situation was different in that the early experimentation was not his last experience.

The homosexual encounter that became the catalyst for Mark's presence on death row began one morning after he took three stimulants. He was using hard drugs less frequently, but he still relied heavily on stimulants, sedatives, and psychedelics like LSD.

The drugs made Mark hyperactive and he became extremely restless. His girl friend wanted him to stay at home with her but he decided he had to leave the house. He commented: "I gotta be alone, man. I can't stand being around people all the time. It just drives me nuts. I gotta have privacy."

Mark decided to join a friend's card party. He knew the other men there, and all of them were similar in temperament. They would play cards, drink, and take pills, talking as little as possible for twenty or more straight hours. It was almost as good as being by himself and it gave him something to do.

The card party ended quickly that day. He left around midnight, then headed for a bar. He had been drinking and smoking marijuana during the game, but he wanted more to drink.

"I sat down in the bar and I remember being about two spaces away from this blond-headed guy. Us two were sort of separated from a group of people who were at the other end of the bar. I ordered a beer and a shot of tequila, which is what I drank."

The other man was a homosexual and apparently very impressed by the "macho" image Mark revealed when he gulped the tequila instead of sipping it slowly. They began talking, the man buying Mark another round of drinks, then Mark treating the two of them.

As Mark was getting ready to leave, another homosexual approached him and struck up a conversation. He began talking about astrology and asked Mark what his birth sign was. Mark said that the ". . . dude was dressed very sharp and didn't have any money. I lent him a cigarette."

Mark agreed to give the second man a ride home. He was living in a vacation home belonging to his parents who were away at the time. He invited Mark in for a drink.

As soon as they got inside, Mark said that the man

> *. . . came to me and makes a pass at me. He came up and puts his arms around my shoulder and when he goes for my crotch, he asks me, "Have you ever done this before?"*
>
> *I didn't answer him. We took off our clothes upstairs*

and I don't remember doing this. I can't picture it in my mind but I knew it happened. We took off our clothes upstairs and went to his bedroom and got into bed. I don't remember much except for I got the picture of me with my arm around the dude's neck and my hand is over his face, closing his nose and mouth. I was in that one position, strangling him.

The next thing that comes to me without my trying to figure it out is being scared. Then the next picture I get is me putting on my clothes in the kitchen upstairs so I know that's where we undressed and put our clothes. I think I might have stayed there an hour after he was dead. . . . Just walked around the place.

Actually, Mark searched the house, but his reasons weren't clear at the time.

Mark's problem was that some of the actions were his own and some were Carl's. Mark had been the one to yield to the homosexual advance initially. However, Carl took over in bed, strangling the other man until he was certain he was dead, then returning control of the body to Mark. Mark was aware of what happened because the dead body was obvious evidence. Yet he genuinely had no knowledge of the actual murder.

Mark went home and found a friend of his, also involved in dope selling, waiting for him. The other youth had fallen asleep but Mark awakened him to tell him about the killing. The friend was quite calm and took Mark to a restaurant. However, Mark was too upset to eat.

Mark was more puzzled by the murder than remorseful. It was like a dream. He related the murder to a television program where someone suddenly "snaps," commits a violent act, then calms down and doesn't really have any memory of the incident.

The more Mark reflected on the incident, the more he came to hate himself and fear what he had become. He realized that he could commit murder without warning or reason. He was terrified of himself and didn't want to go on. "I wanted to kill myself," he told me, adding that he "went over to a friend's house to score enough heroin to kill myself."

Mark never had the chance to overdose. People in the bar remembered him and the fact that he had left with the murdered man. The police caught up with him before he could inject the massive quantity of heroin he had purchased.

Once again I was involved with Mark. The defense attorney wanted my evaluation because I had known Mark over the years. We discussed what he had done, the role Carl played, and other factors related to this most recent crime.

I asked Mark if he wanted me to hypnotize him again so I could help him consciously remember what had happened and thereby try to deal with it. He explained that he had been trying very hard to remember and part of his memory had returned during sleep and meditation. Although he didn't remember the crime, he felt that he did understand what had happened.

"I think if I did kill him, it was because (in my mind) I wasn't killing him. I was killing myself. I think that is the unconscious reason. I wasn't killing him; I was killing me."

Describing his feelings during the murder, Mark said, "At that point I was scared and he was dead; my mother was there and the devil. They were all going to kill me for what I had done. I felt like the devil was there and my mother was there, trying to kill me. All my dreams with her usually end with her trying to kill me."

Mark described his dreams, saying, "The dream started at the point where I felt scared [after the murder]. I was standing there and the dude was dead and my mother was trying to kill me and she killed me. Then I had a gun and started killing everyone and there's all these people all around me, coming in at me, so I managed to get away. I got in the car and I drove it over a cliff to escape them. That was the end of the dream.

"Sometimes I think that's what's in that window," he continued, pointing to a window near his cell. "I think it's my mother trying to kill me inside that window."

It was obvious that one of Mark's problems was the horrible, overriding guilt he continued to feel concerning the accident. I knew he had to find a way to overcome this intense guilt. "Have you ever asked your mother for forgiveness?" I asked.

"Yes . . . No . . ."

"Why don't you try?"

"I . . . I know that she forgives me," Mark said, starting to cry.

"But you don't feel it," I said. "You have to ask for forgiveness before it comes."

Suddenly Mark's emotions got the better of him. His voice seemed to explode as he shouted, "I have! I've asked! I've pleaded! BUT I CAN'T FORGIVE MYSELF!"

"It's not up to you to forgive yourself. It's up to God to forgive you."

> *I know that. I asked for it [the guilt] to be taken away. Please take it away . . . Take it all away. But it doesn't go away. It stays all the time. It haunts me.*
>
> *I'm not haunted with just my mother's death anymore. I'm haunted with everything, every little thing. Everything I think I've done wrong haunts me.*
>
> *There was a girl I met when I was a sophomore [in high school]. She didn't know me. She was going with another guy and then, later in the year, she fell in love with me. But I knew at that point where my life was at. I was self-destructive and anyone who came near me would be hurt. So I didn't want her to come near me and she would come up to me and say, "I love you. Please, I love you." And I would say, "Be my friend," but she didn't want just that and I walked away.*
>
> *That memory still haunts me. All kinds of memories haunt me.*
>
> *Like, I was living with a woman who had a child. I took her kid to the park and spent the day playing with him. He had a great time but his mother wanted to take him out on a lake in a boat and I said, "No, it's too expensive. I can't afford it."*

Mark explained that during that period he couldn't sleep because of the nightmares he repeatedly experienced. "So I ended taking the money I said I couldn't afford to spend on that child and spent it on dope so I wouldn't dream."

Depriving the child filled Mark with guilt that continued

to trouble him. Yet he never experienced these emotions during the incidents, probably because an alter personality took over at those times. He only found out what he'd done later, if he remembered it himself or if someone else told him. Then guilt and remorse would begin to plague him. The one exception was the time of the murder. As he said:

> *Right after I killed the dude, I stood up and looked at the dude and I was afraid of him coming back to life. I told the cops that he was coming back alive and that I was afraid.*
>
> *I* knew *he was dead. I was positive he was dead and at the same time I was afraid he was coming back alive. I don't remember what he looked like or seeing anything at the time. I was scared. Everything was blacked out except the fear and I remembered that when my mother was killed, she was on the highway, torn to pieces, and I knew she was dead. But for a couple of hours I kept begging people to tell me she was dead. Physically I knew she was dead but in another sense I knew she was alive.*

What Mark described was actually a typical grief reaction —denial of a horrible incident one knows about but cannot face. He needed to hear about the death over and over again until he could truly accept the enormous reality of what had happened.

The more we talked, the more Mark's unconscious reasoning became clear. He felt guilt about the homosexual relationship. He knew his mother would have punished him severely. In fact, he felt that if his mother had been alive, she would have imposed the death penalty. As he engaged in sex, he was suddenly his mother and he was surrounded, in his mind, by the devil and numerous other people. Then, in his mental turmoil, he became both the executioner and the victim. The man who died was just a victim of Mark's irrational reasoning. He was not the person Mark thought he was killing.

Yet Mark did kill. No rescuer came forth to stop his hand. Nothing made him pull back at the last minute. It was a deliberate act, although the reality was so twisted in his mind that it was more a suicide than a murder.

After the murder Mark searched the house. He went from room to room, looking for something. The police never learned what he was searching for. He took a few coins, then threw them away. His actions seemed irrational until I questioned him more closely.

"I used to have dreams that my mother was still alive," Mark said. "She was somewhere still alive, her body still moving and I would go and try to find her. She was still alive and she was blaming me for the accident. She kept blaming me for the accident. Over and over again, like a chanting torture. The only way I could stop her from blaming me was to find her and kill her myself. So in my dreams, I'd hunt for her and find her and try to kill her."

Mark admitted that when he searched the house, he was looking for the source of his guilt and his violence. He knew there was "something" outside himself that was responsible for all the horrible events. He frantically tried to locate "it" so he could throw "it" away or destroy "it" and thereby free himself from his tortured guilt.

As we talked, the reason for the earlier arson became clear. Mark was trying to burn anything that might contain the cause of his inner torment. He was convinced that unless he found the specific object that caused his guilt, an object that existed only in his tortured mind, he would never be free from the emotional trauma he had so long endured.

> *I have dreams where I killed myself a lot. I had one dream where I threw myself in hell and I found myself in the blackness. I kept trying to get back to my body. I judged myself. I wanted to die and I said, "Take me, death! Take me, death!"*
>
> *I could hear myself inside my head, screaming . . . screaming to get awake. "Somebody help me! Somebody help me!" Then I fell back into the blackness and I came back and opened my eyes and I felt like lead weights were on my body. I had been asleep for seven hours and was totally exhausted. I could just barely get myself out of bed, but I did because I felt that if I fell back asleep, I'd go back to where I'd been.*

This murder was not the only one Mark/Carl committed. While he was living with his new girl friend, they had a fight and he stomped angrily from the house. During his absence someone broke inside and raped her.

Once again a woman had suffered from an action for which Mark blamed himself. He was convinced that he should have stayed in the house to protect her.

Mark couldn't handle the idea of the rape. He couldn't discuss his feelings with his girl friend, nor had he the courage to talk about her emotions. All he knew was that he was somehow responsible.

Mark coped with the rape the only way he could, using the same kind of denial he had used when his mother was killed. He forced himself to believe that the rape had been the unavoidable consequence of his girl friend's own actions. Perhaps women really liked to be raped and his girl friend had encouraged it. After all, if that was the case, then it would have happened eventually no matter how much time Mark spent at home. Yet he couldn't talk to her about it. His twisted mind formulated an alternative plan.

Mark reasoned that the only way to find out if women enjoyed rape was to test the theory. He approached a friend of his and began discussing the situation. The friend was one of life's losers who spent most of his time burglarizing homes with Mark. The friend was also fascinated with the idea of rape, so the two of them agreed to find out what it was like and what a woman's reaction might be.

The moon was full on the night the two young men actually decided to rape someone. They went down to the pier to drink and take LSD. The drug created hallucinations that intensified their twisted logic. Mark decided that the devil himself had actually entered his mind and body, so he was not in charge of himself. The devil had possessed Mark for his own ends.

They followed several women in their car, finally settling on a particularly stunning woman they saw alone in a coffee shop. They followed her back to an empty apartment and snuck into her apartment through a bathroom window.

They grabbed her before she realized what was happening and began fondling her. His friend had brought along a knife, without Mark's knowledge or consent, which he used to slash at her throat. Then he stabbed her chest, cutting the ribs so that she bled profusely while she screamed and fought.

Mark's friend enjoyed the girl's suffering. He raped her, then let Mark take his turn. When Mark was finished, he figured the girl had suffered enough. He took the knife and stabbed her through the heart. This final wound proved fatal.

For some reason that was never made clear to me, Mark and his friend decided to take home some souvenirs. Perhaps Mark subconsciously sought punishment and knew that taking such items might help get them caught. They took a pocket calculator, some pantyhose, and one or two other items, all of which were readily identifiable and could easily link them with the crime.

Mark then drove to his friend's house, where they awakened the friend's roommate. They were extremely excited and pleased with themselves and gave the calculator to the friend, who, in turn, gave it to his girl friend. He also told his girl friend about the incident and she urged him to report the murder to the police.

The police investigated unsuccessfully for over a month and were only able to link Mark with the crime after he'd been arrested for the homosexual murder. While Mark was in jail, the boy who had received the calculator decided to tell the police what he knew.

He and his girl friend were afraid to go directly to the police because they did not want Mark's friend to think they were "squealers." Instead, the couple started a public fight, knowing that the police would be called to settle the disturbance. When the officers arrived, the boy became abusive, taking swings at the police. He was immediately taken to the station, which was precisely what he wanted. Once there, he readily told his story concerning the murders. He figured that he could always say that the police "forced" the information from him, that he had not volunteered it freely.

There was little question about Mark's mental instability and his attorney advised him to plead not guilty by reason of insanity. However, he was sentenced to death for committing first-degree murder against the woman and, in a second trial, was convicted of second-degree murder against the homosexual. He was moved to death row, then eventually shifted to a different section of the penitentiary when a Supreme Court ruling abolished California's death law. Mark's sentence was commuted to life imprisonment.

I wish I could report that Mark received the psychiatric treatment he needed. However, this was not the case.

Mark was upset by my intention to appear at his trial. The idea that he was a multiple personality did not concern Mark. He did not care if I brought that fact to the jury's attention and he did not feel there was anything wrong with that. He was concerned that I might mention the Peeping Tom episodes. Within the prison population this type of sex crime had a stigma attached to it that murder did not. Mark seemed to fear that I might blackmail him with this terrible secret, even though the reality of murder was, to everyone else, far worse. His secret never came out since I didn't testify in court, and Mark went to prison unembarrassed.

Once Mark was sentenced, my contact with him ended for all practical purposes. There are professional therapists attached to every prison system but their roles are limited. Certainly no one is going to bother spending state money to treat a multiple personality on death row. Thus, this highly troubled youth is destined to spend the rest of his years as a victim of an unusual type of madness. It is one of the tragedies of our penal system, and the situation is unlikely to improve in the near future since Mark's crime was murder. If Mark had been a shoplifter or alcoholic offender like other multiple-personality patients of mine, this would not have been a problem. But when murder is involved, public sympathy disappears and personal fear predominates.

I interviewed Mark several times while I still had access to him, and I was amazed at how much I was able to learn. I have already mentioned my surprise at learning that rescuer personalities do not always stop the killer instinct of the violent alter personality. In Mark's case, all the personalities—and I identified at least four—were aware of the murders, including the original Mark personality who had apparently stopped involving himself with the outside world at age fourteen when Mark witnessed his mother's death. All the personalities had been observers during the murder; none of them had tried to stop the killing. Apparently, Mark was without a conscience.

I had very mixed emotions about Mark. The crimes he had committed were horrible, yet they weren't the actions of a rational individual. He had to be separated from society, yet with treatment there was a chance a very different individual might emerge.

I didn't feel the same sense of responsibility or failure I had felt in Carrie's case. Mark and I simply hadn't had enough contact to permit treatment. I had done what I could, given the limits I was placed under, and I felt only sadness that another human being was not given the chance to live a normal life.

Perhaps I was able to remain more detached in Mark's case because I was facing a serious personal crisis as well at that time. Although I had a realistic attitude about Mark, I wasn't as successful with some of my other multiple-personality patients. The stress of my unusual practice had begun to wear me down. I had to maintain a calm exterior in the midst of violent, irrational behavior. I was concerned about my patients' welfare; their suicide attempts; the midnight calls that might be a life-or-death crisis or, frustratingly, the spoiled rantings of someone who wanted to be pampered by his or her doctor. I thought I was coping very well, despite pressure from patients as well as other doctors, the peer review committee, and even political involvements within the various psychiatric associations to which I belonged.

On December 19 the stress reached its peak. I had spent an hour and a half with my most difficult multiple-personality patient, using a routine to try to ease some of her current anger. Although she felt better when we were through, both my nurse and I were emotionally exhausted. Before leaving the hospital, I had to spend a few minutes with a different patient recording a routine medical history, and I noticed that my writing was small and awkward. It was a handwriting change that always accompanied my periods of extreme exhaustion.

I went home and crawled into bed. Several moments later I felt a wave of nausea, and I rushed to the bathroom and immediately vomited blood. I fell into the shower stall next to the toilet, calling weakly for my wife.

Another doctor, a close personal friend, met me at the Emergency Room of the hospital where I had been the chief of the department of psychiatry. He immediately recognized that I had a bleeding ulcer and used a stomach tube to pump ice water into my body in a desperate effort to stop the bleeding. I had lost so much blood already that a few more hours without treatment would have meant my death. I spent the rest of the night in Intensive Care and was transferred to a private room for the next ten days.

I should have known I had an ulcer, because of the stress I was under and the way my body had been responding for the past several months. I often had severe stomach cramps that stopped when I ate some food. I assumed that the cause was hunger since the pain went away each time I ate. However, my medical training was thorough enough for me to realize, if I had wanted to, that an ulcer was also a likely cause. The acid build-up in the stomach lining was causing the pain, and the food was absorbing the acid rather than letting it continue to eat away the stomach lining. Obviously I hadn't wanted to face the reality of my condition and the restrictions it would place on my life.

The ulcer was only one manifestation of the pressures I had been living with. I was also in a state of extreme physical and emotional exhaustion. While I was in the hospital I found myself unable to stop crying. Every time I tried to talk to someone, about anything, my voice would choke and tears would begin streaming down my face. Actually, this is a fairly typical symptom of this kind of exhaustion, but my emotional state was such that I was unable to think logically and realize that complete rest would restore my normal equilibrium. At the time I was terrified that I'd be unable to continue my work.

My profession demands that I be on top of every situation. To my patients I am all-wise—the ideal father image, always in control, with the "right" answers for every problem. Of course, this isn't really the case, but it is an image my patients need to believe in if therapy is to be successful. If I couldn't even greet them without bursting into tears, my usefulness as a professional was over. I had either to overcome this reaction or to give up the work I loved. And I couldn't face that alternative. It seemed worse than death would have been.

Eventually, logic reasserted itself and I came to terms with my illness. I accepted the necessity of slowing down and reducing my load of professional obligations. I also accepted the ulcer and the restrictions it would impose. I was simply glad to be alive and have the chance to continue my work. My family helped enormously.

They rallied around me. They came to the hospital for Christmas dinner, wheeling me into the cafeteria so we could all be together. We all shared the traditional turkey with all the trimmings, and the occasion had an emotionally uplifting effect on my spirits.

I was away from the office a total of six weeks, during which I caught up on my paper work and began eliminating some of my many commitments. I resigned from various committees and even took myself off Emergency Room call service for six months. This service meant that I, along with other local doctors, was on call for any psychiatric emergency that might occur at the hospital. Although I hated to give up such work, I realized that I couldn't handle the additional pressure until I was completely well again. Six months later I went back on call.

In one sense, the ulcer was good for me. It made me face and deal with some of the stresses I had been trying to avoid admitting. At the same time, I realized that no matter what happened to me, I would always have to put my patients ahead of myself. I could not turn my back on the personal vows I had made after Carrie's death. I would get out of psychiatric association politics and avoid, wherever possible, all obligations that did not relate to primary patient care. But I was a doctor in search of the secrets of the mind, and I had already uncovered aspects that had never been reported before. I knew that whenever my life was over, all that I had gained would be but a fraction of the knowledge left to learn. Yet my patients were constantly helping me discover bits and pieces of the jigsaw puzzle that is the mind. Whatever small fraction of knowledge I introduced would add to the total human understanding, and I could not reduce my active pursuit of the cause and cure of one of our most unusual mental problems.

Chapter 8

Possession and the Spirit World

I have touched briefly on the subject of spirit possession earlier in this book, specifically in Carrie's case. At that time, after much soul-searching, I decided to take a radical step and perform an exorcism to help rid Carrie of certain overwhelming fears. My procedure was successful, although I wasn't sure how or why it worked. I do not know whether Carrie was genuinely possessed, or simply thought she was; I do know that my "exorcism" proved to be a valuable therapeutic tool.

I assumed, of course, that Carrie would be my first and last encounter with spirits and exorcisms. Originally, I viewed the idea of possession with as much skepticism as my colleagues, and I was glad to dispense with a procedure that created so much controversy and criticism.

However, in the years that followed, many of my other multiple-personality patients exhibited similar symptoms. Repeatedly, I encountered aspects or entities of their personalities that were not true alter personalities. It is of course possible that multiple personalities are particularly susceptible to such delusions. But in many of these cases, it was difficult to dismiss these unusual and bizarre occurrences as mere delusion. In the absence of any "logical" explanation, I have come to believe in the possibility of spirit possession.

The entities to which I refer simply could not be considered genuine alter personalities. As we've seen, an alter personality serves a definite and practical purpose—it is a means of coping with an emotion or situation that the patient cannot handle. It might express anger, pain, sexuality, joy, love, or fear, but there is always a logical reason for the alter personality's "existence" and a known time of creation. Some alter personalities, for example, are created for one situation and disappear immediately. If a patient doesn't know what to have for dinner or which movie to see, he or she might create a personality specifically to make that decision. This is often a typical pattern for many multiple personalities, since it is their primary method of coping with any crisis, regardless of its relative importance.

Thus, the discovery of an entity who doesn't serve any recognizable purpose presents a diagnostic problem. Interestingly enough, such entities often refer to themselves as spirits. Over the years I've encountered too many such cases to dismiss the possibility of spirit possession completely.

The case of Elise is perhaps a classic example. I first began treating her when she was twenty-four years old. At the time she had sixteen alter personalities and a hierarchy of five Inner Self Helpers. Each served a specific purpose in her life and each was created to handle a trauma that Elise herself couldn't face. Eventually, I was to discover more than double this number, since Elise coped with all the problems in her life by creating alter personalities. She was, in fact, typical of the pattern described above. She would often create a personality simply to handle a relatively minor decision or problem.

During one of our sessions I put Elise under hypnosis to discuss the recent death of her grandmother. It was a trauma she hadn't been able to handle, and we were exploring new ways of coping. When we had finished, Elise suddenly faded out and a male named Dennis took over.

The appearance of a male alter personality in a female's body didn't surprise me. It was a situation that had occurred before. It is most common in female patients who believe their fathers wanted a son instead of a daughter. In order to win their fathers' love, such women often create a male alter personality to become the "son" their fathers want.

I immediately began questioning Dennis, trying to learn

everything I could about him. At the end of our session, however, it was obvious that Dennis wasn't an alter personality; he served no purpose, nor could I pinpoint the time of his "birth." By his own admission, he remained with Elise only because he was sexually aroused by Shannon.

Shannon *was* one of Elise's alter personalities, or so I thought at the time. She had been created when Elise, then twenty-two, lost her baby. The trauma was so horrifying that Elise had let Shannon take over. Shannon returned every October and controlled the body until March 31—the anniversary of the baby's long illness and eventual death. Shannon was emotionally strong and self-assured, well able to function despite grief. And Dennis had fallen in love with her.

I was completely taken aback by this story. I had never encountered a situation where one alter personality fell in love with another; in fact, it simply didn't seem possible, even within the confines of the bizarre world of multiple personality. Yet there was no other logical explanation for Dennis's existence. Elise had never shown any lesbian tendencies, nor did she need a "man" to handle any of the crises in her life. Without guidelines, I really didn't know what to do, so I tried to reason logically with Dennis.

Logic has always been a useful tool in dealing with an opposite-sex alter personality. In one case of mine, the "man" was out on an occasion when my female patient had to use the bathroom. She was in a store at the time and, naturally, the "male" in charge of the body went to the men's room. After arguing with one of the store clerks, "he" finally stepped up to the urinal and discovered that "his" penis was missing. It was instant castration in "his" eyes and the effect was horrifying. "He" was not quite ready to face the fact that perhaps the patient really was a woman, but "he" became so weak that he receded into the mind for a prolonged period. By the time "he" came out again, the patient was so close to fusion that it was a relatively simple matter to eliminate the male alter personality.

I asked Dennis how he expected to have sex with Shannon, hoping my logic would upset him. He explained, however, that when Shannon was in charge of Elise's body, Dennis would get inside whatever man she was dating. When Shannon went to bed with that man, Dennis would be inside him, enjoying the sensation.

When Dennis finally went under, Shannon came out and complained about him. She confirmed everything he had said, and reported that he liked to make his presence known by pinching her immediately after intercourse. Normally, none of the men she slept with pinched her. This occurred only when Dennis was inside a particular man. It was his "calling card" and she hated him for it.

I was completely baffled by this turn of events. I had been trying to understand and define Dennis as another type of alter personality, yet all evidence seemed to contradict this view. I thought it was possible that an alter personality could exist without a known purpose or time of origin, but it was completely impossible for an alter personality to enter someone else's body. But both Shannon and Dennis admitted that he did this frequently.

I knew something was wrong. The idea that an alter personality could leave the body at will is nonsense. There is a sound psychological reason for the creation of an alter personality. Either the stories I heard about Dennis were not accurate or he simply was not an alter personality.

Finally, I decided to interview Elise's Inner Self Helpers, who had an overview of the situation. They insisted that Dennis was not an alter personality. He was a spirit and would not be eradicated by the normal process of fusion.

Despite my previous encounter with spirits, I wasn't quite ready to believe this assessment. Although I could accept the possibility of the spirit world on an intellectual level, I wasn't able to relate to the concept emotionally. I decided to interview Dennis again, tape recording everything he had to say. I wanted proof so that I could report this startling information to others, and I wanted to be able to listen to the conversation again, to try to come to grips privately with what I'd inadvertently discovered.

Our conversation was general at first. Then I asked him how he had originally become acquainted with Shannon.

"I saw her out and I thought, 'Far out, hey, that's what I want!' " he told me.

"Where were you at the time?" I asked.

"Out and about, doing my thing."

"In somebody else or just floating about between people?" I didn't really know what to ask or even what I meant by the question. Since he claimed to be a spirit, I assumed it was possible for him to be away from the body.

"I was in somebody else."

"Why didn't you stay in that somebody else?"

"Because she [Shannon] didn't happen to like him."

I laughed at that remark and asked Dennis if he had ever found a male body to use as a permanent home. Reluctantly he admitted he hadn't. Shannon had never settled down long enough. However, he liked the potential. He said, "If she'd find someone she'd like, far out! Man, I'd just pop myself in there. But she won't. She's too picky."

Dennis continued, "She doesn't want to get married. All she wants to do is—what she calls it—be her own person."

Dennis then explained that he had been in two or three men, each of whom had had relations with Shannon. We discussed his attitude toward the main personality as well as the other alter personalities discovered to date, and none of them interested him. He only wanted Shannon. She was the only one he loved, despite the fact that they were all creations of the same mind.

Eventually I asked Dennis if he had ever had his own body. "A long time ago," he said with a touch of sadness.

"What did you do?"

"I was a stockbroker, till somebody shot me."

"Where were you living?"

"Down south somewhere—Louisiana."

"How old were you when you were shot?"

"I was about seventy."

"Why were you shot?"

" 'Cause somebody pointed a gun at me and it went off!"

"I understand that, but I was wondering . . ."

"I was being robbed!"

"Oh, okay. Were you a successful stockbroker?"

Dennis indicated that he had had only moderate success. He did enjoy the gambling aspect of the field, however.

"When were you shot . . . what year?"

"Nineteen forty-something. I don't remember."

"I've always wondered what it's like to be shot and die."

"It hurts. The dying part . . . that's not bad. It's getting there that hurts."

"What's it like once you have gotten there?"

"It doesn't hurt."

"What kind of an experience did you have when you realized you didn't have that body to cart around?"

"Shocked the hell out of me!" he said. Then he added, "Especially when I realized they were going to bury me. God, can you imagine the name that they gave me?"

"Name?"

"Julius."

"Julius what?"

"That you'll never know."

"We have a lot of people buried in the cemetery out there," I added. "I always wonder what happens to their spirits when they go into the ground."

"I'm not one of them."

"I know you're not."

"It's cold down there, and I decided, you know it's really weird, watching your own funeral. Why are we talking about this? Let's talk about Shannon. I really dig her."

"All right. Tell me what you like about her."

"Everything."

"Let me ask you, as a stockbroker, did you have a lively romantic life too?"

"Yeah. My wife didn't like it all that much."

"Kind of frustrating?"

"For her, yeah."

"How about for you? Did you have girl friends on the side to make up for it?"

"Yeah, a couple."

"I just wondered how come you're so hep on sex right now? Is this making up for lost time?"

"Because I missed a lot of lost time. I mean, the dudes that I got into . . . You would not believe. God, Frankenstein looked better than them, even in the movies."

"Didn't you pick them on purpose?"

"No. It just happened."

"Were you born into them or did you come into them as an adult? Did you borrow their bodies like you did Elise's?"

"No, I kind of latched onto them."

"Do you come in and control somebody, possess them and control them, and they do what you want until you leave?"

Dennis said that he could, that he had never been reborn into a new body. He explained that he was assigned to each body he entered and went with people who had a definite identity. He never was clear about who assigned him, though. He described some of the bodies he had entered:

"He was a coal miner with the ugliest wife in town. I can't even remember her, I stuck around for such a short time. I didn't even pay attention. Once I sized up the situation, I said, 'No way.' I split after about five days."

"Where did you exist during those five days?"

"Inside the body."

"Once you left, where did you go?"

"Outside the body." He continued, "Then I got some dude up in Frisco who was a sailor in the early sixties, I think. No, it was before that. But God, he could get the cutest girls, and they were foxy chicks."

"Sailors are sometimes pretty lucky."

"Unfortunately, he died of spinal meningitis, which really was a bummer." Dennis spent a total of approximately three years with him, staying with him until he died. It was the last body he had used on a regular basis before joining Elise and meeting Shannon, "the love of my life."

Dennis claimed that he entered Elise in 1968, five years before I met him. He admitted to participating in a gang rape Elise endured about that time as well. He had left Elise's body in order to enter the bodies of the men raping her.

We talked about Dennis's relationship with Shannon and I explained that she disliked him. "She says you're ugly. She said, 'Have you seen his face?' I said, 'No, I haven't.' " Then I added, "If she keeps rejecting you, how come you're so persistent?"

"Because I like her."

"At a certain point you really ought to give up and try somebody else."

"I'm persistent."

"I know that, but you're wasting your own time, don't you think?"

"Not as long as I can screw her. I screwed her a couple of times . . . more than a couple of times."

Dennis faded out shortly after that and Shannon returned to complain about the situation, adding that no one in the body really liked Dennis. Despite all my efforts, I was unable to find a more plausible explanation for his existence than the spirit theory.

Eventually I talked to the major Inner Self Helper within Elise. This ISH was also a male, but his purpose was clear and he had a definite date of origin. He told me that Dennis had come into Elise's body when she and a group of her friends, all in their late teens, had experimented with black magic. He had entered her mind while she was trying to open herself to Satanic possession. I was told that Dennis could be removed from the body the next day if I handled the matter alone, standing well away from Elise while I worked so there was no risk that Dennis would enter my body.

Elise was hypnotized the next day, then taken back to the day she had engaged in the occult ritual with her friends. Elise told me that she was about to join some friends in the woods and hear a lecture about the spirit world by someone named Michael, who was supposedly a spirit himself. I didn't know what to make of all this, although it was apparent that she believed she was genuinely practicing occult rituals at that time. She felt she was evil and part of a group of other evil beings.

I tried to reason with Elise as I might have done had she really come to me in 1968. I told her that what she was doing could be emotionally destructive. I also pointed out that God was love; her description of Michael's teachings didn't relate to love. Since Elise frequently talked about seeking God's love, I thought this might have some impact, even though, for the moment, her mind was five years in the past. However, she was skeptical and demanded that I prove how her actions could hurt her.

I took out my tape recorder and played the tape of my

conversation with Dennis. I wanted her to know what would happen to her if she continued to dabble with the occult. Initially, because Dennis's voice was deeper than her own, she had trouble identifying with it. However, when Dennis mentioned her name she became upset.

Elise wanted additional proof, so I called on one of her Inner Self Helpers to guide her. I knew from experience that a patient's mind can supply the necessary answers at times, and I hoped that would happen.

Suddenly everything changed. Elise's eyes, which had been closed, opened. A voice, unlike all the others I had heard, said, "And that is how I began." Instead of exorcising Dennis, I was confronted with another spirit. This spirit was female, and further questioning elicited the facts that her name was Michelle and that she was responsible for the dead batteries in the first of two tape recorders I eventually had to use to replay Dennis's tape.

Michelle informed me coldly that she was against God. She knew she would have to leave Elise one day, as would Dennis, but she vowed that she wouldn't go without a fight. She also said that Shannon couldn't fuse until Dennis left and he would remain as long as Shannon was present.

Elise was in the hospital during this period and I really had no idea what to do next. My interview had ended inconclusively as far as I could tell. However, that evening Elise began switching personalities every thirty seconds. The nurse who witnessed the event was frightened and called me at home. Naturally I returned to the hospital as quickly as possible.

The nurse understood my treatment techniques and managed to talk to two of the Inner Self Helpers before I arrived. She was told that it was time to eliminate Dennis and Michelle.

As soon as I arrived, the nurse and I took Elise to a grassy spot on the hospital grounds where she could move about without being hurt. She slumped to the ground and suddenly began screaming, "Get out of my body! Get out! Get out!" A different voice shouted, "I'm not going to leave!" Then Elise screamed, "If there is a God, help me!" Seconds later she became unconscious.

She awakened a few minutes later, but she was not the

same person who had entered the hospital. Instead, it was Elise as she had been when she was twenty-two, and the discovery came as a shock. She started to become hysterical, then her mind switched and she let an alter personality take over. This personality, Sandi, returned quietly to the ward. Along the way she described seeing three dark blue spheres with black linings and gray edges, one larger than the other two, apparently leaving Elise's mind.

The following morning I talked with an Inner Self Helper who said that Michelle, Dennis, and one other female spirit whom I had never met had all left. This is what Sandi had seen. She also said that Dennis's story about his origins was correct, and that she, the Inner Self Helper, had more work to do before completely eliminating all the spirits affecting Elise's mind.

I didn't know quite what to say or do next. Although I can accept the possibility of life after death and the existence of a spirit world, it is truly shocking to witness such an encounter. Nothing in the psychological literature could account for what I had seen. Even my own theories about alter personalities no longer seemed valid. I wanted to discuss the matter, but with whom? I had tapes of Dennis and the corroboration of the nurse who had witnessed some of what went on. Yet this entire experience was so foreign to me that all I could do was watch in awe and hope that I was heading in the right direction.

I continued working with Elise during her stay in the hospital. I used hypnosis to regress her, and we dealt with some of her early traumas. I showed her new ways of coping and generally followed the routine that had proven successful with my other patients.

Then one day I was summoned by the nurse. I met with an Inner Self Helper who told me that preparations had been made for Shannon's elimination. I was to oversee the actual process. I was told that Shannon was actually the spirit of Elise's baby who had died a few months after birth. Shannon was not an alter personality created to cope with the trauma of that loss. Shannon was actually the baby's spirit, and Elise would have to eliminate Shannon.

I took Elise to a vacant conference room where furniture

had been removed. She fell on the floor and, for the next half hour, rolled about, hallucinating Shannon as her enemy. First I heard Shannon's voice shout, "I'll kill you if it's the last thing I do!" Then Elise yelled, "Get out of me! Get out of me!"

Elise's hands went to her face as she tried to claw her own neck and strangle herself. She fought for control, shouting, "I do believe in God! I do!" She writhed and rolled, fighting something inside her, while the nurse and I kept her from hurting herself.

Suddenly Elise stopped. She stretched out her arms and shouted, "I demand that you leave!" Then all was quiet; the battle was over. She slumped to the floor unconscious, then awakened a few minutes later. An alter personality took charge and got her back to her room and into bed.

I thought the problem was over. I thought that whoever or whatever Shannon might have been was gone, but I was wrong. The next day a greatly subdued Shannon appeared to tell me that she was, indeed, the spirit of Elise's baby. She was also now ready to leave. "I'll be dying in a few hours," she said. "I'll belong to another child, beyond Elise, in another time."

Shannon continued: "I've given up my battle. I don't know why. She will have no dreams about me and will barely remember the child. I would never have been able to help you. I'd stop them [the alter personalities] from trying. I was jealous that Elise was working toward something good. When she is well, she will be a big asset to you. . . . I caused a great deal of harm and hurt. In a way I won and also lost. I'll be back again. Elise is important to you; she sees you as a person trying to help lots of people. Her belief in God is becoming strong."

I was trying to understand Shannon's role so I asked what she did for Elise. She replied, "I did the things that were right for her, like getting rid of her husband. Someday she will learn to handle her own hurts. She will not go through the hell I put her through. I showed her what hell could be. I wanted to get at Sandi the most. She had all the abilities I wanted. Help her get her memory back. She will never think of me as a person."

Shannon continued talking, making what amounted to a farewell speech. Finally, she shook my hand solemnly and said, "After Elise takes her nap, I will be gone."

Elise awakened with amnesia, but gradually regained most of her memory over the next three days. However, she returned home with no memory of the "battle" with Shannon.

What did it all mean? I don't know. Dennis and the others certainly did not fit any of my theories about alter personalities, yet that does not mean my current conclusions are correct. I'm certain only that these entities seemed to exert an influence over Elise and, with their absence, she was able to get well.

Sophia, another one of my patients, had an even more bizarre experience. Her therapy had gone very well, and I anticipated a successful final fusion. However, I was amazed to discover that two personalities remained even after final fusion. Their names were Mary and Maria and neither served any recognizable purpose, nor seemed in any way typical of a genuine alter personality. Mary wanted to be a nun but couldn't since Sophia was married. Maria enjoyed socializing in very moderate fashion. She never got drunk or exhibited the wild sexual behavior common to such alter personalities. Both of them enjoyed life but refrained from engaging in any activity that might harm Sophia or affect her adversely.

After repeated questioning under hypnosis, I was given information about Sophia's birth. I regressed Sophia to the time of her birth and listened in amazement to her description.

Her mother had given birth at home and had had triplets. The doctor who delivered the babies was also her mother's lover and apparently didn't want the children to be born. He smothered the first two but wasn't able to kill Sophia because a neighbor chanced to drop by the house during her arrival. Fearing discovery, the doctor let Sophia live.

According to what Sophia said under hypnotic age regression, the spirits of all three babies had been hovering over the bodies, waiting to enter after each baby was delivered. But the first two spirits were left homeless after the murders. Sophia's spirit entered the live baby's body, then became concerned that the two hovering spirits of her dead sisters might be lonely. She invited them to share Sophia's body, which they gratefully did.

After ten days of therapy Sophia informed me that she no longer needed Mary and Maria within her. I placed a bottle in each of her hands, then put her into a trance. Using a deep, professional voice, I ordered her to send Mary out her left arm, into the bottle in her left hand, and Maria out the right arm, into the other bottle. Sophia grunted, groaned and squirmed in her chair, apparently reaching into the depths of her being to bring forth the spirits. When she relaxed, the spirits were gone. I removed the bottles and awakened Sophia from her trance.

After giving her a chance to rest, I put her in a trance and tried to call Mary and Maria in the same manner I had used during the many weeks of therapy. They did not respond, nor did they ever appear again. They were gone, although I will never know how or why.

Another case of possession involved a twenty-four-year-old patient of mine named Francine who was hospitalized because she could no longer function at all. Only one week earlier Francine had revealed two alter personalities in my office, one a violent man hater, and the other a weak, rather ineffectual rescuer.

Francine had been raised by her Episcopalian grandmother and Pentecostal mother. During her early years Francine had been surrounded by relatives who spoke in tongues during the Pentecostal church services. Later she rebelled and became a heroin addict, spending a year in a drug abuse rehabilitation center operated by a Pentecostal minister who spoke in tongues and cast out demons as part of his therapy.

While Francine was in the hospital, she had to attend a group therapy session. During one session she became highly agitated and realized that her violent alter personality was taking over. She ran to her room and stared out the window, where she began to see demons. The nurse tried desperately to calm her but had no luck. Eventually I was called to the hospital. Unfortunately there was nothing I could do to help her relax.

Suddenly Francine began repeating syllables over and over

as though speaking a poem in a foreign language. It was a consistent wording and I suspected that she was speaking in tongues.

Slowly Francine's voice rose louder and louder. Then she turned abruptly toward the window, raised her arms, and shouted, "In the name of Jesus, I banish you. I banish you from this room!" She continued shouting the words over and over again. Then, almost as abruptly, she stopped, lay down on the bed, and went to sleep.

The episode was repeated two or three more times in the days that followed. Her ISH told me that Francine really had been possessed and her actions had cast out the demons.

Is there true spirit possession? I don't know. However, I have developed some theories based on my experiences and I have identified five levels of spirit possession, at least in my practice.

The first type of "possession"—Grade I possession—is easily understandable in psychiatric terms. It could also be labeled obsessive-compulsive neurosis, a term with which many of my colleagues feel comfortable. In such cases the patient is controlled by an idea, obsession, involuntary act, compulsion, or addiction to alcohol or drugs.

A woman with an obsessive-compulsive neurosis came to me for treatment of depression and a hand-washing compulsion. Many years ago water had splashed from a public toilet into one of her eyes, causing conjunctivitis. Ever since then she avoided public toilets because she believed that another such incident would cause blindness. Her fixed idea about the danger of public toilets greatly hampered her social life. She had to give up her former job as a legal secretary and she could not take advantage of any of the cultural events in town.

Almost every psychiatrist has treated this type of neurosis. In some cases physical damage can result from the compulsive act and the patient may suffer severe harm or even accidental death.

Many psychotherapists agree that it is extremely difficult to treat such a person with normal in-office therapy, and these patients are often encouraged to participate in group therapy or to join groups patterned after Alcoholics Anonymous. Only when the patient realizes that he is being dominated by an addiction or obsessive idea that could potentially destroy him, can he find the strength necessary to change. "Exorcism" is self-initiated and supported by the group. Once it occurs, the rebuilding of a new life begins.

Alcoholics who have joined AA talk about their powerlessness when confronted by alcohol. They speak of seeking help from God or a power greater than themselves. They also support one another, eventually developing alternative ways to cope with their problems. The concepts they follow, such as AA's twelve steps, are thus adaptable to other addiction problems. (Gamblers Anonymous, Pills Anonymous and numerous others.)

Multiple-personality patients are the victims of Grade II possession. Grade II possession is the result of the influence of a negative alter personality developed by a person with a hysterical personality structure. One young man created an imaginary friend at the age of nine while hiding under the bed to escape another of his mother's regular, violent tirades. This dissociated mental creation evolved into an alter personality who hated all women and considered them sexually debased. Eventually he raped and killed six young women in two states. At the same time, his primary personality held down a responsible job, lived with a girl friend, and helped raise their young son. When he weakened in any way, the alter personality came out and killed another woman. The primary personality was totally amnesic for all these episodes until a psychiatric investigation was conducted under hypnosis. He was found to be a modern Dr. Jekyll and Mr. Hyde with absolutely no recollection of the periods of murderous activity.

In many cultures the alter personality would be considered a classic example of an evil spirit invading the body of this decent young man. However, deep hypnosis showed very clearly the psychosocial roots of his mental splitting. The way this alter personality was able to handle the repressed aggression against his mother was clearly demonstrated. With adequate information from his unconscious, there is no need to invoke supernatural explanations.

Grade III possession occurs when the controlling influence seems to be the mind of another living human being. At this level witchcraft may be involved. For example, a very Americanized Mexican woman, who did not believe in witchcraft, came to my office complaining of depression and physical weakness. These symptoms had developed just after her nephew was killed in an automobile crash the night before his wedding. The young man's mother (my patient's sister) blamed the patient for his death. The sister and their mother visited a local black witch and had been observed by other family members performing black magic rituals aimed at harming my patient. Under hypnosis I asked about the cause of the problem and a voice came forth, identified itself as the sister of my patient, and explained the root of her hatred for my patient. She admitted that she had caused all of the suffering my patient had endured over the past year. After I told her to return to her own body and leave my patient alone, my patient awoke with no memory of the hypnotic session although she felt relieved of her symptoms.

I was unable to follow up on this case so I do not have an accurate diagnosis of my patient's mental condition. But I do know that my patient considered witchcraft pure superstition and personified the typical sophisticated American housewife. Both her sister and mother were still very superstitious and fully believed in native Mexican folk rituals involving witchcraft. They bought black candles and other paraphernalia from a local witch and regularly performed such rituals. They believed fully that one mind could adversely affect another from a distance. The voice had identified herself by name as the sister, and she hated my patient because she was so well liked by everyone while the sister was despised by most who knew her. This was the sister's way of punishing my patient for her popularity.

Grade IV possession is control by the spirit of another human being.

One young lady, who also had multiple personalities, found herself compelled to walk from her home to the local harbor without knowing why. When she finally regained consciousness and control of her body, she went to a phone and called a friend. I saw her at home shortly thereafter, induced hypnosis, and asked what was responsible for this odd behavior. A voice came forth and claimed to be the spirit of a woman who had drowned herself in the surf of the Atlantic Ocean while searching about the boats in the harbor for her husband and children, who had deserted her. She stated that she had taken over this patient's body to continue the search. After she agreed to leave the patient, the patient ceased to be interested in walking near the water.

This patient was well known to me and I was acquainted with all of her alter personalities. She had often been "taken away" by entities who claimed to be either good or evil spirits, and this was corroborated by her helper alter personalities. This particular spirit had not completed a necessary function at the time of her demise, namely, finding her family. The spirit did not accept the reality of her death and had to take over the body of a susceptible person who lived near a harbor.

Grade V possession is control by a spirit that has never had its own life history and identifies itself as an agent of evil. I once saw a young man who had been injured at work when a piece of machinery fell on his head. He had had several subsequent convulsive seizures but neurological evaluations did not show injury sufficient to explain the cause of the seizures. He also began hearing a voice that told him that he was shortly going to die. During hypnosis, I asked the reason for these symptoms.

A voice came forth, claiming to be the "devil." This "devil" claimed to have entered the man several years before, when he was serving with the U.S. Army in Japan. The man had run into a burning house to rescue a Japanese occupant and when he did, an explosion blew him out of the house. The man was hospitalized for months and was very unhappy about the poor quality of his medical care. This "devil" claimed to have entered the body at the time of the fire. He also claimed responsibility for the machinery accident and all subsequent physical and mental symptoms.

I secured a consultation with a local priest, who also met this same "devil" simply by reciting certain rituals. The priest believed that this "devil" was really an evil spirit and eliminated him with various rituals.

The rules of exorcism laid down in 1614 in the Roman

Catholic *Rituale Romanum* were designed to deal with these evil forces. Only the power of God and his angels can conquer such entities. In the true case history on which *The Exorcist* is based, the boy involved was first thought to be possessed by the spirit of a dead aunt. Only when the priests started the formal rites of exorcism did they report that demonic possession had begun. It took six weeks of day-and-night exorcism to bring the boy back to health.

My own sense of ease with these concepts is probably a result of my religious training and beliefs. Futhermore, I simply cannot dismiss the experiences of my patients—the entities I discovered in many of these cases simply do not reflect the classic, accepted pattern of multiple personality. Nor am I the only psychiatrist to have made such startling discoveries. Other psychiatrists have reported similar experiences, and I have corresponded with many professionals who have come to similar conclusions about the origins and purpose of alter personalities. These professionals have treated patients dominated by "someone" who simply doesn't fit this pattern. And in many cases, they don't know what steps to take.

I can only reiterate my own belief—that an effective doctor must use whatever methods benefits the patient most. In my own cases this has often entailed the utilization of techniques that are bizarre, unorthodox, and even religious in nature. But these methods have successfully cured many patients, and the patient's welfare must be the only concern.

Are patients really possessed at times? I don't know. Perhaps my cures result from making the right moves for the wrong reasons. Perhaps I am not exorcising a spirit but, rather, "lucking" into a less than conventional approach to alter personalities. At this point I can only describe the experiences I have encountered. Hopefully, in the years ahead, either I or some other researcher will be able to develop concrete answers for this fascinating, highly controversial aspect of the human mental condition.

Chapter 9

Conclusions

When I first began to work with multiple-personality patients, I assumed that if I ever wrote a book on the subject, I would be able to provide a brilliant summation pinpointing the causes and cure of this unusual mental illness. I believed that several years of experience would be sufficient to develop a real understanding of this problem. My work, and the work of other doctors, would confirm the theories and conclusions I'd developed from my early cases, and we would formulate a quantitative method for treating multiple personality.

However, experience has tempered this rather optimistic viewpoint, and I now realize that my study of multiple personality is still in its infancy. It is an illness of incredible complexity and variety. No sooner have I confirmed one concept—the existence of the Inner Self Helper, for example—than I am forced to discard another cherished theory. Easy answers simply are not possible.

Several years have passed since that awful night when I first learned of Carrie's death. Hundreds of patients have passed through my office door, a number of whom shared her special problem. Each new case has broadened my perspective and increased my knowledge, but I'm very much aware of the frontiers that remain uncharted.

Despite the frustrations and setbacks I've faced, I am determined to learn as much as I can and to share whatever knowledge I have with others. Perhaps this determination is due, in large part, to Carrie's death. If I can pass on what I've learned to another doctor, I may help prevent another needless suicide. At the very least I can give other doctors the benefit of my experience and provide the kind of guidelines I didn't have when Janette—my first multiple-personality patient—entered my office.

Thus, I have attempted to write and lecture on the subject whenever I can. I have given lectures in Sweden and conducted educational programs at the annual convention of the American Psychiatric Association. This kind of exposure has also led to increased hostility from some of the other doctors in the small California community where I formerly practiced.

My critics could not dispute the severity of my patients' illness, nor could they deny the success I had in curing so many. But I continued to utilize methods that were unconventional at best, and the pressures on me grew. Eventually I found that I had too few patients to justify the expense of running a private practice and I could no longer rely on referrals from the doctors uneasy with my work. Nor could I turn my back on the vow I'd made to myself after Carrie's death. I had to continue in my attempt to understand and conquer this bizarre mental disorder.

I solved my dilemma by giving up my private practice and moving to another city. I began working in a clinic, eliminating the pressure and expense of private practice without sacrificing my work. It has been a satisfying decision. However, I've been careful to handle the unusual aspects of multiple personality only in the presence of other professionals. When another doctor actually witnesses a patient switching personalities or hears an ISH talk about spirit possession, my theories no longer seem as unorthodox or "far out."

However, I realize that many of these theories may be shattered in the years ahead as more work is done in this field. The challenge of formulating a methodology and the necessity of discarding it when it is no longer applicable is an integral part of such pioneering work. I have already found it necessary to revise some of my early theories, and I'm sure this process will continue as long as my work continues.

For example, I had previously thought that every alter personality had a uniform moral code. Each personality represented a moral choice. There were "good" personalities and "evil" personalities, but the differences were never ambiguous in any way. However, I recently encountered what appears to be an alter personality without any sort of moral code. She is sometimes "good" and sometimes "bad." She seems unable to make any moral judgments about her actions, and this is unique in my experience. Such a personality could, for example, work in a department store as a security guard, defending management's property with her life if necessary. At the same time she could shoplift an item on her lunch hour and see nothing wrong with her action. I don't know why such a personality developed in this way, although I am certain she is a true alter personality. All I can do is proceed with treatment and hope to learn exactly how this personality was created. Perhaps then I will have answers that clarify this fascinating new development.

Another one of my pet theories that I've been forced to revise was the idea that alter personalities are formed as a result of childhood experiences. I had assumed that it took a period of time and prolonged interaction with abusive and/or uncaring parents before some trauma triggered a child's first split. However, I now know that it can sometimes happen at the moment of birth.

In one case, according to the Inner Self Helper, the patient's mind was so extremely powerful in its psychic ability that it split into two parallel personalities at the moment of birth. The personalities operated side by side, sharing abilities in unusual ways. They both took art training, for example, and one would paint the top half of a picture, then black out and allow the other personality to finish the bottom half.

Critics of multiple-personality diagnosis contend that alter personalities can be created by suggestion. This is quite true. Most of these patients are hysterics and they are easily suggestible, especially under hypnosis.

I have always tried to be extremely careful in my work, but in at least two cases I was responsible for "giving birth" to an alter personality. The first case was Carrie's; she created a personality to handle the shock of diagnosis when I explained her condition for the first time. This was not a deliberate creation, but it was a situation I could have avoided had I realized just how unstable she was at that time.

The other case was deliberate. One of my patients entered the hospital in such emotional turmoil that most of the normal personalities running the body could not handle the task safely. The one personality who was responding properly was an eight-year-old child who wasn't mature enough to remain in charge. I talked with the Inner Self Helper, who can create personalities when necessary. She agreed to form a new personality who was socially adept, non-neurotic, fearless, and fully aware of the existence of all the other personalities. This "individual" assisted me throughout therapy and eventually fused to become part of the cured patient.

I do not yet fully understand how an Inner Self Helper can create an alter personality. In this particular case the ISH formed a personality with interesting contrasts. The main personality had never done well in school and had no interest in reading. She was a drug abuser at one time and frequently used sleeping pills and tranquilizers as a means of coping with her problems. She seemed content to be more of a passive observer of life, although she engaged in fairly frequent sexual activity.

The alter personality created by the ISH was a self-composed, intelligent, mature woman who did not believe in indiscriminate affairs or drug use. She was also somewhat of an intellectual, regularly borrowing books from my library because she had an insatiable curiosity about everything.

As the final fusion between the patient and her ISH-created alter personality took place, the patient's liftstyle changed. She lost interest in indiscriminate sex and eventually settled into a relationship with a man who had no interest in drugs. The patient began reading, even though she had previously been only semiliterate. The best parts of the created alter personality became an integral aspect of the patient.

Although these examples prove that the development of a methodology for dealing with multiple personality is difficult at best, I have refined a treatment approach that appears to work in almost all cases, regardless of the individual differences in patients. This therapeutic method consists of eight intertwining stages which occur in the following order:

1. *Recognition of the existence of the alter personalities.*
2. *Intellectual acceptance of this condition.*
3. *Coordination of alter personalities.*
4. *Emotional acceptance of multiplicity.*
5. *Elimination of persecutors.*
6. *Psychological fusion.*
7. *Spiritual fusion.*
8. *Post-fusion experience.*

I have already covered the first seven areas in some detail throughout the book. The last point is still being explored by myself and other psychiatrists because so little is known about the needs of a post-fusion patient. Guidelines must be established to help these patients readjust to a normal life.

We do know that most patients continue to face old problems for an indefinite period after fusion. In many cases legal charges must be faced and resolved. Marriages may be broken or vows renewed. New occupational directions may be necessary. Many patients move to new surroundings so that they can take on normal social roles without the stigma of illness following them. Life continues to present problems, but they can cope in a more effective and conscious way.

And I continue my work; exploring, learning, trying to help people who once thought they were hopeless. I also continue to pass along what I have learned so that the mistakes I made with Carrie will not be repeated by equally "green" psychiatrists with similar patients. I have been allowed to enter realms of the mind seldom, if ever, studied and I know I have only touched the surface of this new frontier.

Often I feel a great sense of pride in my accomplishments. At other times I am terrified by how little I know while probing the most powerful force at our disposal, the human mind. Yet little by little, patient by patient, day by day, I am advancing and learning. ·

Janette chose to live. Carrie chose to die. I can't alter those facts, but as I apply my increasing knowledge, I can only hope that my present and future patients will take the option of life and move forward through God's healing power. The mind is our greatest resource, and I am determined to help those in turmoil find peace and cope with life as whole, rational, emotionally stable individuals.